Reassuring Teachings on Death

BRUCE E. DANA

Published by Ringmasters Jewelry and Gift

Table Contents

Defining Death

What does the word *death* **mean to you? Why** is it that all mankind must die? If you truly knew there is a glorious life following death, would that give you more comfort and peace? With the spirit as our guide, let us learn gospel truths about this *inevitable event* that allows us to gain eternal life.

REAL EMOTIONS EVOKED

From personal experiences, as well as speaking with many individuals, I have learned this verity: Repeatedly, death comes as unexpectedly as the first frost of winter. It is broadly perceived as a stranger who suddenly appears without warning, evoking pangs of sorrow and emptiness for those left behind. The loss and hurt are real, its intensity varying only between individuals and family members.

Many times, death silences the laughter of little children. It takes away those who are midway through life's journey, and it comes to the aged. For those individuals who experience great suffering and illness, death comes as an angel of mercy. Yet, even when the elderly or infirm have found merciful relief, their loved ones are rarely ready to let them depart.

It is important to emphasize that death eventually comes to all mankind (See 1 Corinthians 15:22; 2 Nephi 9:6; Alma 12:23-24). It is no respecter of age, gender, or race. It is appropriately stated that all people are only one breath away from death.

It is natural that we mourn for those loved and taken by the heavy hand of death. One of the deepest expressions of pure love is mourning. Knowing that we would experience the loss of loved ones, the Lord revealed this knowledge to the Prophet Joseph Smith: "Thou shalt live together in love, insomuch that thou shalt weep for the loss of them that die" (Doctrine and Covenants 42:45). Though death evokes a variety of emotions, it should be viewed as a natural consequence of mortality. Eternal perspective provides peace "which passeth all understanding" (Philippians 4:7).

In one of his excellent writings, then Elder Russell M. Nelson, of the Quorum of the Twelve Apostles, clearly and concisely tells that this life can be compared to a "three-act drama." He further explains that "Act one began long ago in premortal realms... We were spirit sons and daughters of our loving Heavenly Father in Heaven, eager for an opportunity to come to earth to receive a body. That body was to be created in the image of our divine parentage. It was to serve as the tabernacle for our eternal spirits.

"Through the miracle of birth, spirit children of God obtain their physical bodies." Next, he quotes this meaningful scripture from the Book of Mormon:

"There was a space granted unto man in which he might repent; therefore this life became a probationary state; a time to prepare to meet God; a time to prepare for that endless state which has been spoken of by us, which is after the resurrection of the dead (Alma 12:24)."

He then says that "While...in act two [which is mortal life on this earth], each human soul consists of two component parts: an eternal spirit and a physical body." Later, he explains that our bodies "were built in such a way that they were subject to illness, injury, aging, and death." Speaking plainly and truthfully, he states, "We start to die the moment we are born." He then asks and answers his own question, "Why? The reason is simple. Our Heavenly Father wants us to return to him. He gave us life, and he provided the means by which we could return to him... Birth is the gateway to mortal life; *death is the gateway to immortality and eternal life.*" [1]

Later in this work, we will discuss act three—life after death.

<u>TWO KINDS OF DEATH</u>

Two kinds of death are referred to in the scriptures. One is *spiritual death,* when an individual is cast out of the presence of the Lord, to die pertaining to righteousness and the things of the Spirit. The other is *physical death,* which is caused by the separation of the spirit from the mortal body. As recorded in the New Testament, it is aptly written that "the body without the spirit is dead" (James 2:26).

Regarding physical death, the scriptures generally refer to it as the *natural* or *temporal death.* The Prophet Joseph Smith received this revelation:

"But, behold, I say unto you that I, the Lord God, gave unto Adam and unto his seed, that they should not die as to the *temporal death,* until I, the Lord God, should send forth angels to declare unto them repentance and redemption, through faith on the name of my Only Begotten Son.

"And thus did I, the Lord God, appoint unto man the days of his probation—that *by his natural death* he might be raised in immortality [living forever as resurrected beings] unto eternal life, even as many as would believe." (Doctrine and Covenants 29:42-43. Italics added)

<u>UPLIFTING DESCRIPTIONS OF DEATH</u>

Regarding the natural or temporal death, President Brigham Young, second President of the Church, made these informative remarks: "In many places in the scriptures, the separation of the body and spirit is called death; but that is not death in the strict sense of the term; *that is only a change.*" [2]

Giving additional information, President Heber C. Kimball, a counselor to President Brigham Young, gave this positive description:

"We say the dead have departed this life as though they had departed to some other life. This, however, is not so; *dying is like going from one room to another*, or from one part of the earth to another, *the life still exists though the body decays*, but the life which dwelt in it is indestructible." [3]

At the funeral of Sister Elizabeth H. Cannon, President Wilford Woodruff, then President of the Quorum of the Twelve Apostles, expressed this enlightening view:

"On such occasions when mourning the loss of departed friends, I cannot help but think that *in every death there is a birth*: the spirit leaves the body dead to us, and passes to the other side of the [veil] alive to that great and noble company that are also working for the accomplishment of the purposes of God, in the redemption and salvation of a fallen world." [4]

Looking at death logically, Elder Orson F. Whitney, of the Quorum of the Twelve Apostles, explained: "It never crushes me when a dear one departs; for I have learned some things about death that prevent me from taking gloomy and hopeless views of the subject... Everything around us, animate or inanimate, obeys a great natural law and returns to the place from which it came. We ourselves are subject to the law. *It is just as natural to go out of this life as it is to come into it*; and what we call *death is the doorway out of the world, as birth is the doorway into it*." [5]

With an eternal perspective, President Joseph F. Smith, sixth President of the Church, stated these great truths: "Although painful in the extreme to those who must suffer the departure of dear ones, *death is one of the grandest blessings* in the divine economy; and we think children should be taught something of its true meaning as early in life as possible. We are born that we may put-on mortality, that is, that we may clothe our spirits with a body. Such a blessing is the first step toward an immortal body, and the second step is death. *Death lies along the road of eternal progress;* and though hard to bear, no one who believes the gospel of Jesus Christ, and especially in the resurrection, would have it otherwise. Children should be taught early in life that death is really a necessity as well as a blessing, and that we would not and could not be satisfied and supremely happy without it." [6]

Speaking of the joyous reunion we will experience, Elder Franklin D. Richards, of the Quorum of the Twelve Apostles, assuredly stated: "Latter-day Saints who live their religion having a testimony of Jesus, have no fear of death. We look at it as but *a stepping stone* from one apartment of God's great creation to another. *When we leave our kindred here, we will be united with a greater number there; and some of our very dearest kindred are there waiting for us. Wives, parents, fathers, and mothers, brothers and sisters, children of all ages await our presence there."* [7]

From these informative and uplifting statements, natural or temporal death has appropriately been defined by the Lord's chosen servants as follows:

(1) A gateway to immortality and eternal life
(2) A change of condition
(3) Like going from one room to another

(4) A birth into the world of spirits

(5) A doorway out of this world

(6) Is one of the grandest blessings

(7) A stepping stone to a reunion with departed loved ones

<u>MORE DEFINITIONS</u>

The following definitions come from Richard M. Eyre's work, *The Birth We Call Death*:

"Seneca said: 'The day which we fear as our last is but the birthday of eternity.'

"Samuel T. Coleridge said: 'Death but supplies the oil for the inextinguishable lamp of everlasting life.'

"Benjamin Franklin wrote: 'A man is not completely born until he is dead.'

"Rossiter W. Raymond said: 'Life is eternal and love is immortal; and death is only a horizon, and a horizon is nothing save the limit of our sight.'

"William Penn: 'For death is no more than a turning of us over from time to eternity.'" [8]

The following is a story told at a funeral about a sailing ship: "In a beautiful blue lagoon on a clear day, a fine sailing ship spreads its brilliant white canvas in a fresh morning breeze and sails out to the open sea. We watch her glide away magnificently through the deep blue and gradually see her grow smaller... as she nears the horizon. Finally, where the sea and the sky meet, she slips silently from sight; and someone near me says, 'There, she is gone!'

"Gone where? Gone from sight—that is all. [Note these words:] She is still as large in mast and hull and sail, still just as able to bear her load. And we can be sure that, just as we say, 'There, she is gone! another says, 'There she comes!'" [9]

From these definitions, particularly the sailing ship story, we can relate that when an individual experiences mortal death, family and friends will sadly say, "He or she is gone!" However, when this individual enters the spirit world, loved ones will joyfully exclaim, "Here he or she comes!"

<u>SPIRIT WORLD</u>

When physical death occurs, a spirit that is temporarily housed in a mortal body departs and goes into a place called the spirit world. This teaching is verified by the declarative words spoken by Alma, as recorded in the Book of Mormon:

"Behold, it has been made known unto me by an angel, that the spirits of all men [mankind], as soon as they are departed from this mortal body, yea, the spirits of all men, whether they be good or evil, are taken home to that God who gave them life. . . that the spirits of those who are righteous are received into a state of happiness, which is called paradise, a state of rest, a state of peace. . ." (Alma 40:11-12. Italics added).

From Alma's explanation, an individual learns that *paradise is a temporary home*, designated as the space appointed between death and resurrection, when eventually a person's spirit and body will once again be united, never to be separated. (See Alma 40:20-23; Doctrine and Covenants 88:15-17; Alma 11: 43-44. Italics added).

Speaking as a "linguist," the Prophet Joseph Smith stated that "Hades, the Greek, or Sheol, the Hebrew, these two significations mean a world of spirits. Hades, Sheol, paradise, spirits in prison, are all one: it is a world of spirits." [10]

PARTIAL JUDGMENT

In LDS beliefs the following truth is written: When entering the world of spirits, *"we undergo a kind of partial judgment, after which our spirit goes either to spirit prison or to paradise.* Spirit prison, or hell, is a temporary abode of disembodied spirits at various levels of preparation, knowledge, and goodness who are given an opportunity to acknowledge their wrongdoings on earth, repent of sin, learn the principles of the gospel of Jesus Christ, choose whether they will receive that gospel, and prepare for resurrection." [11]

<u>VISION OF PRESIDENT JOSEPH F. SMITH</u>

In section 138 of the Doctrine and Covenants, it records a vision given to President Joseph F. Smith, sixth president of the Church, on October 3, 1918. It was given to him six weeks before he passed away.

Elder Bruce R. McConkie, of the Quorum of the Twelve Apostles, summarized what transpired: "President Joseph F. Smith saw in vision the visit of the Lord Jesus Christ in the spirit world. He saw that the Lord appeared to the righteous; that among the wicked and ungodly he did not go; and that he organized the work there and sent messengers to preach to all the spirits in prison."

He both saw and testified:

"I beheld that the faithful elders of this dispensation, when they depart from mortal life [by death], continue their labors [missionary work] in the preaching of the gospel of repentance and redemption, through the sacrifice of the Only Begotten Son of God, among those who are in darkness and under the bondage of sin *in the great world of the spirits of the dead*. The dead who repent will be redeemed, through obedience to the ordinances of the house of God [temples]. And after they have paid the penalty of their transgressions, and are washed clean [through vicarious baptism performed in temples], shall receive a reward according to their works, for they are heirs of salvation." (Doctrine and Covenants 138:53-58). [12]

LOCATION OF THE SPIRIT WORLD

President Brigham Young asked this searching question: "Is the spirit world here?" Answering, he revealed this knowledge: "It is not beyond the sun, *but is on this earth* that was organized for the people that have lived and that do and will live upon it." [13]

Elder Parley P. Pratt, of the Quorum of the Twelve Apostles, also wrote: "As to its location, it is here on *the very planet where we were born.*" [14]

In complete harmony with these two statements, then-Elder Harold B. Lee, of the Quorum of the Twelve Apostles, stated: "The spirit world isn't on another planet millions of miles away. *The spirit world is right here on this earth.*" [15]

As the spirit world is on this earth, it is natural to ask, "Why can't we see individuals who have gone into the spirit world?" To answer, we turn to Elder Alvin R. Dyer, who then was an Assistant to the Quorum of the Twelve Apostles, for explanation: "*There is a veil between the one sphere and the other* which renders the spiritual sphere invisible to the temporal. To discern beings or things in the spirit world, a person in the flesh [mortality] must be quickened by spiritual element; the veil must be drawn, or the organs of sight, or of hearing, must be transformed, so as to be adapted to the spiritual sphere." [16]

Elder Russell M. Nelson expressed this truth: "Other prophets and Church leaders have also stated that the spirit world is on or near the earth. *Its location may be less important than its actuality.* All who pass through the gateway of death go immediately into the spirit world." [17]

How a Spirit Leaves Its Mortal Body

IT IS NATURAL TO WONDER HOW A SPIRIT LEAVES its mortal body and goes into the spirit world. Speaking at a meeting held in the Tabernacle at Salt Lake City, Utah, in 1860, Elder Orson Hyde, of the Quorum of the Twelve Apostles, spoke early in the meeting. He briefly spoke of an article that was published about Mr. Davis. President Brigham Young was the next speaker and provided additional information:

"Brother Hyde... referred to a statement made by Andrew Jackson Davis. He placed himself in a [mental] state beside the bed of a sick person and observed the spirit of a lady leave her body. *He saw the spirit ascend from the head of the mortal tenement*—saw it walk out into the open air in company with another spirit that came to escort her away. They appeared to him to ascend an inclined plane, and continued to walk away until they were out of sight." [18]

Expressing his personal view, President Young said: "Do you not believe that your spirit will be in existence after it leaves the body? *I care not whether it goes out from the head or from some other portion.*" [19]

From these statements, it is evident that both Elder Hyde and President Young were familiar with a published article about an experienced observed by Mr. Davis. In addition, both these Church leaders felt a need to talk about what Mr. Davis witnessed.

When he briefly spoke of the experience of Mr. Davis, Elder Hyde made this qualifying statement:

"With regard to the operation of death, I do not know that I will exactly endorse the principle, but I will take up what Andrew Jackson Davis says. *It is rather singular, and I don't think it is very far from the truth.*" [20]

SILVER CORD

During his remarks, President Young said that Mr. Davis observed that after the spirit was fully out of the body, *"he saw as it were an umbilical cord that yet retained the spirit to the body; and that when that was separated, the spirit was free, and the body was consigned to dissolution."* [21] Some people believe this "umbilical cord" is called a *silver cord.*

To support that belief, they quote two verses written in the Old Testament of the Bible: *"Or ever the silver cord be loosed,* or the golden bowl be broken, or the pitcher be broken at the fountain, or the wheel be broken at the cistern. *Then shall the dust return to earth as it was: and the spirit return unto God who gave it."* (Ecclesiastes 12:6-7. Italics added).

Pertaining to these scriptures, an acknowledged Bible commentary says: "Commentators have differed much as to the interpretation of this passage. It has been taken by many as a description of the gradual failing of one bodily organ after another till death supervenes [follows]." Further, "and the golden bowl of the lamp of life is broken, and the silver cord, by which it is suspended, loosed..." [22]

From published statements, individuals have described the "silver cord as being smooth, very long, very bright, like an elastic cable made of light, about an inch wide...and attached to one of several possible locations on the physical body." When death finally occurs, this silver cord is severed and "the spirit body is released from being attached to the physical body." Some believe that this "silver cord is our spirit body's 'lifeline' to our physical body in the same way that our umbilical cord is our 'lifeline' to our mother's body during the birth process." [23]

It is important to emphasize that some individuals might classify these statements as interesting speculation, not supported in Latter-day Saint commentary. Whatever one's view, these statements are presented only for consideration.

Returning to the story briefly related by Elder Orson Hyde of what Mr. Davis observed, Elder Hyde concluded his remarks by saying:

"If that live image did come out as he represented, that is the part that shall never die; *and whether it [a spirit] passes out in that particular form, matters not*; we know that it does escape and live forever." [24]

At the conclusion of President Young's remarks as to the statement made by Mr. Davis, President Young stated: "*Whether this be true or not, it is as certain that the spirit leaves the body...* When it leaves the body, it dwells in the spirit world until the body is raised up by the power of God." [25]

Though Elder Hyde and President Young spoke of a "*rather singular*" experience observed by Mr. Davis, both Church leaders stated that it does not matter how the spirit leaves its mortal body. All that is revealed, and perhaps all that we need to know at the present time on this intriguing subject is this: When physical death occurs—as explained by Alma, in the Book of Mormon—*a spirit that is temporarily housed in a mortal body departs and goes into a place called the spirit world* (Alma 40:11-14).

Death Of Infants And Children

SPEAKING AS A FORMER HEART SURGEON AND AS A member of the Quorum of the Twelve Apostles, Elder Russell M. Nelson wrote these assuring words: "I also learned that every now and then, the Lord takes these special spirits back home to him early, as if to spare them some of the weighty trials that mortality would have brought. Repeatedly I have seen that happen. Spiritually mature and sensitive children are called by their Creator prematurely (according to human criteria) to pass through the gateway to immortality and eternal life."

He then quotes these prophetic words: "The Prophet Joseph Smith expressed himself on this subject. He said, 'The Lord takes many away even in infancy, that they may escape the envy of man, and the sorrows and evils of this present world; they were too pure, too lovely, to live on earth; therefore if rightly considered, instead of mourning we have reason to rejoice as they are delivered from evil, and we shall soon have them again.'

"He [the Prophet] further explained: 'All children are redeemed by the blood of Jesus Christ, and the moment that children leave this world, they are taken to the bosom of Abraham. The only difference between the old and dying is, one lives longer in heaven and eternal light and glory than the other, and is freed a little sooner from this miserable wicked world.'" [26]

Elder Nelson then writes this verity: "Lamenting parents may safely place their trust in the hands of God, who lent them each precious little life in the first place. Though parental grief is real, normal, and divinely encouraged (see D&C 42:45), it can be eased to a tolerable degree by sincere gratitude—and understanding. Those little ones are children of our Heavenly Father, too." [27]

Directing his remarks to those individuals who have had infants and children pass away, President Joseph F. Smith wrote these encouraging words:

"Under these circumstances, our beloved

friends who are now deprived of their little one, have great cause for joy and rejoicing, even in the midst of deep sorrow that they feel at the loss of their little one for a time. They know he [or she] is all right; they have the assurance that their little one has passed away without sin...They will inherit their glory and their exaltation, and they will not be deprived of the blessings that belong to them."

President Smith then provided these assuring words:

"Joseph Smith declared that the mother who laid down her little child, being deprived of the privilege, the joy, and the satisfaction of bringing it up to manhood or womanhood in this world, would, after the resurrection, have all the joy, satisfaction and pleasure, and even more than it would have been possible to have had in mortality, in seeing her child grow to the full measure of the stature of its spirit."

Speaking of personal loss, he honestly declared: "With these thoughts in mind, I take consolation in the fact that I shall meet my children who have passed behind the veil; I have lost a number, and I have felt all that a parent can feel, I think, in the loss of my children. I have felt keenly, for I love children... I feel thankful to God for the knowledge of these principles, because now I have confidence in his word and in his promise that I will possess in the future all that belongs to me, and my joy will be full. I will not be deprived of any privilege or any blessing that I am worthy of and that may be properly entrusted to me." [28]

AGE OF ACCOUNTABILITY

The Prophet Joseph Smith revealed: "I also beheld that *all children* who die before they arrive at *the years of accountability*, are *saved in the celestial kingdom of heaven*." [29]

What, then, is the age of accountability?

In answering, then Elder Joseph Fielding Smith, of the Quorum of the Twelve Apostles, declared: "The Lord has placed... *the age of accountability at eight years*... Now he has himself arbitrarily declared that. I did not set the age. I accept it because the Lord set the age, and this is the law." [See Doctrine and Covenants 68:27]. [30]

Accordingly, every child, regardless of what dispensation, where it is born, the color of its skin, whether born in or out of the covenant, comes into this world innocent in its infant state.

In a letter from Mormon to his son, Moroni, these enlightening and true doctrines are taught:

"For, if I have learned the truth, there have been disputations among you concerning the baptism of your little children. . . . I desire that ye should labor diligently, that this gross error should be removed from among you."

Note these words: "I inquired of the Lord concerning the matter. And the word of the Lord came to me by the power of the Holy Ghost, saying: Listen to the words of Christ... I came into the world not to call the righteous but sinners to repentance... little children are whole, for they are not capable of committing sin; wherefore the curse of Adam [accountability that comes with the fall of Adam] is taken from them in me, that it hath no power over them... that it is solemn mockery before God, that ye should baptize little children... their little children need no repentance, neither baptism... little children are alive in Christ [saved by His atonement]." (Moroni 8: 5-12; read entire chapter].

Continuing, Mormon declares: "For awful is the wickedness to suppose that God [saves] one child because of baptism, and the other must perish because he hath no baptism. Wo be unto them that shall pervert the ways of the Lord after this manner, for they shall perish except they repent. Behold, I speak with boldness, having authority from God; and I fear not what man can do... And I am filled with charity, which is everlasting love; wherefore, all children are alike unto me [equal worth]; wherefore, I love little children with a perfect love; and they are all alike and partakers of salvation" (Moroni 8:15-17).

With these truths stated, we return to the words previously spoken by President Joseph F. Smith regarding the death of young children: ". . . they [parents and family members] have the assurance that their little one has passed away without sin... They will inherit their glory and their exaltation, and they will not be deprived of the blessings that belong to them." [31]

__STATURE OF CHILDREN__

Prior to being born in mortality, spirit children of our Heavenly Parents have reached the stature of adulthood. Regarding the spirit and how it affects the growth and size of the physical body it is temporarily housed in, we rely on the wisdom of Elder Orson Pratt, of the Quorum of the Twelve Apostles:

"The tabernacles of both animals and vegetables continue to grow or increase in size, until they attain to the original magnitude of their respective spirits, after which the growth ceases. When the spirit first takes possession of the vegetable or animal seed or embryo, it contracts itself into a bulk of the same dimension as the seed or tabernacle into which it enters:... [Note these words:] Spirits, therefore, must be composed of substances, highly elastic in their nature, that is, they have the power to resume their former dimensions, as additional matter is secreted for the enlargement of their tabernacles. It is this expanding force, exerted by the spirit, which gradually develops the tabernacle as the necessary materials are supplied." [32]

From this explanation, it is apparent that the spirit is quite elastic and that growth depends on receiving sufficient nutrients.

DEPARTED CHILDREN

At times, spirits of departed infants and children have appeared in the form of an infant or child to those individuals who would be able to identify them in that manner. President Jedediah M. Grant, a counselor in the First Presidency to President Brigham Young, was able to see his daughter as a tiny baby while his spirit was in the spirit world. At President Grant's funeral, President Heber C. Kimball, a counselor in that same First Presidency, revealed this information:

"During brother Grant's brief sickness... I went to see him one day last week ... I laid my hands upon him and blessed him, and asked God to strengthen his lungs that he might be easier [to breathe and speak], and in two or three minutes he raised himself up [from his bed] and talked for about an hour... telling me what he had seen and what he understood...

"He said to me, brother Heber, I have been into the spirit world two nights in succession... He saw his wife; she was the first person that came to him. He saw many that he knew, but did not have conversation with any except his wife Caroline. She came to him, and he said that she looked beautiful and had their little child, that died on the Plains, in her arms, and said,

"Mr. Grant, here is little Margaret; you know that the wolves ate her up, but it did not hurt her; here she is alright."' [33] More on this occurrence will be given later.

In harmony with this story, President Joseph F. Smith declared:

"If you see one of your children that has passed away it may appear to you in the form in which you would recognize it, the form of childhood." [34]

Regarding a deceased child coming as a messenger from the presence of God, he provided this explanation: "But if it came to you as a messenger bearing some important truth, it would perhaps come as the spirit of Bishop Edward Hunter's son (who died when a little child) came to him, in the stature of full-grown manhood, and revealed himself to his father, and said: 'I am your son.'

Providing additional information, President Smith revealed: "Bishop Hunter did not understand it. He went to my father [Hyrum Smith, the brother of the Prophet Joseph Smith] and said:

'Hyrum, what does that mean? I buried my son when he was only a little boy, but he has come to me as a full-grown man—a noble, glorious, young man, and declared himself [as] my son. What does it mean?'

"Father [Hyrum Smith, the patriarch] told him that the Spirit of Jesus Christ was full-grown before he was born into the world; and so our children were full-grown and possessed their full stature in the spirit, before they entered mortality, the same stature that they will [have] after they have passed away from mortality, and as they will also appear after the resurrection, when they have completed their mission." [35]

Likewise, Elder Melvin J. Ballard, of the Quorum of the Twelve Apostles, related an appearance of his deceased son and gave this description:

"I lost a son six years of age, and I saw him a man in the spirit world after his death." [36]

STATUS OF CHILDREN IN RESURRECTION

Regarding the status of children in the resurrection, President Joseph F. Smith spoke this uplifting doctrine:

"[The Prophet] Joseph Smith taught the doctrine that the infant that was laid away in death would come up in the resurrection as a child; and, pointing to the mother of a lifeless child, he said to her: 'You will have the joy, the pleasure, and satisfaction of nurturing this child, after its resurrection, until it reaches the full stature of its spirit.' There is restitution, there is growth, there is development, after the resurrection from death. I love this truth. It speaks volumes of happiness, of joy and gratitude to my soul. Thank the Lord he has revealed these principles to us." [37]

He says that in "1854, I met with my aunt, the wife of my uncle, Don Carlos Smith, who was the mother of that little girl that Joseph Smith, the Prophet, was speaking about and bore testimony to me that this was what the Prophet Joseph Smith said." President Smith further said that he spoke and received statements from others who were at this same meeting. "Just a little while later... Presidents Woodruff and Cannon [of the First Presidency] approved of the doctrine. . ." [38]

This teaching is clarified and supported by the teaching of then Elder Joseph Fielding Smith, of the Quorum of the Twelve Apostles: "When a baby dies, it goes back into the spirit world, and the spirit assumes its natural form as an adult, for we were all adults before we were born.

"When a child is raised in the resurrection, the spirit will enter the body and the body will be the same size as it was when the child died. *It will then grow after the resurrection to full maturity to conform to the size of the spirit.*

"If parents are righteous, they will have their children after the resurrection. Little children who die, whose parents are not worthy of an exaltation, will be *adopted* into the families of those who are worthy." [39]

He further declared: *"Of course, children who die do not grow in the grave. They will come forth with their bodies as they were laid down, and then will grow to the full stature of manhood or womanhood after the resurrection,* but all will have their bodies fully restored. [40]

Then these comforting and assuring teachings: "When a person rises in the resurrection, his [or her] body will be perfect... Bodies will come up, of course, as they were laid down, but will be restored to their proper, perfect frame immediately. . . . *If there has been some deformity or physical impairment in this life, it will be removed"* [41] [See also Alma 11:42-45; 40:22-23].

<u>DECEASED CHILDREN TO CHOOSE MATES IN MILLENNIUM</u>

Elder Joseph Fielding Smith recorded: "We have people coming to us [leaders of the Church] all the time just as fearful as they can be that a child of theirs who has died will lose the blessings of the kingdom of God unless that child is sealed to someone who is dead. They do not know the wishes of their child who died too young to think of marriage, but they want to go straight to the temple and have a sealing performed. Such a thing as this is unnecessary and, in my judgment, wrong.

"The Lord has said through his servants that during the millennium those who have passed beyond and have attained the resurrection will reveal in person to those who are still in mortality all the information which is required to complete the work of these who have passed from this life. Then the dead will have the privilege of making known the things they desire and are entitled to receive. In this way no soul will be neglected and the work of the Lord will be perfected." [42]

From David J. Ridge's study, it is written: "Since they will be exalted, we know that they will be married. They will be given the opportunity in the afterlife, somewhere after they die and before the day of final judgment, to associate with others, [choose] a mate, and to have someone on earth get sealed for them, by proxy, in a temple, during the Millennium." [43]

After my wife delivered a beautiful, healthy baby girl, she shared a room in the hospital with a grieving mother whose child had just died. I sincerely desired to give comfort to this mother by explaining that she would have the blessing of raising her child after the resurrection. Being justifiably upset, she glared at me and angrily exclaimed, "But that does not fill the void in my arms right now." I learned a valuable lesson: Unless guided by the Spirit, avoid expounding doctrine, but have sincere empathy and love for a grieving individual.

We conclude with these promising words from Elder Nelson:

"Parents who have surrendered the sweetest and smallest flowers from the family's garden need to remember our loving Heavenly Father. He has promised a special reward to those who now suffer in silence, who spend long days and longer nights through their trying times of bereavement. Our Creator has promised glory. He said, 'For after much tribulation come the blessings. Wherefore the day cometh that ye shall be crowned with much glory; the hour is not yet, but is nigh at hand' (D&C 58:4) That promised glory includes the blessing of reunion with each little child who has left the family circle early to help surviving members of the family to draw nearer to God. Those little children still live and are a heritage of the Lord." [44]

Stillborn Children

FROM THE DAYS OF ADAM TO THE PRESENT, MYRI-
ads of women have experienced an early miscarriage of a fetus or have had a Fallopian tube pregnancy that has resulted in a miscarriage. When a fetus—described as a developing human—is born dead, it is defined as a stillbirth.

Whatever medical terminology is used, this event has caused many family members of The Church of Jesus Christ of Latter-day Saints to wonder about the status of the fetus. These searching questions are generally asked: (1) Did the fetus become a living soul—wherein the spirit and the body were united? (2) Will a stillborn or miscarried baby be resurrected? And (3) Will parents eventually be able to raise these little ones?

The revelations given to the Prophet Joseph

Smith have not explained why these events take place in the life of women, or what transpires with the fetus in the eternal plan of our Heavenly Father. However, leaders of the Church have either spoken or written encouraging and uplifting counsel on this subject.

Concerning when a spirit enters its mortal body, President Brigham Young expressed the belief that "when the mother feels life come to her infant, it is the spirit entering the body." [45] [See Luke 1:39-41].

There are various views on when quickening occurs before a child is born in mortality. Some believe a spirit enters at the time of conception, and the spirit makes the fetus develop in its mother's womb. Others believe that the spirit does not enter until the child takes its first breath of life. Admittedly, the revelations have not defined when the spirit enters the body.

Regarding the death of a fetus, President Brigham Young said:

"But suppose an accident occurs and the spirit has to leave this body prematurely, what then? All that the physician says is—'it is a still birth,' and that is all they know about it; but whether the spirit remains in the body a minute, an hour, a day, a year, or lives there until the body has reached a good old age, it is certain that the time will come when they will be separated, and the body will return to mother earth." [46]

RESURRECTION OF STILLBORN CHILDREN

Elder Joseph Fielding Smith stated, "There is no information given by revelation [about] the status of stillborn children. However, I will express my personal opinion that we should have hope that these little ones will receive a resurrection and then belong to us. I cannot help feeling that this will be the case.

"When a couple have a stillborn child, we give them all the comfort we can. We have good reasons to hope. [Note these words:] Funeral services may be held for such children, if the parents desire. Stillborn children should not be reported nor recorded as births and deaths on the records of the Church, but it is suggested that parents record in their own family records a name for each such stillborn child." [47]

In the February 2025 General Handbook, published by The Church of Jesus Christ of Latter-day Saints, it is written: "28.3.1. **Children Who Died Before Birth (Stillborn and Miscarried Children)** Temple ordinances are not needed or performed for children who die before birth. For more information, see 38.7.3)." It is further written: "28.3.2 **Children Who Died Before Age Eight.** Little children are redeemed through the Atonement of Jesus Christ and 'saved in the celestial kingdom of heaven' (Doctrine and Covenants 137:10). For this reason, no baptism or endowment is performed for a child who died before age 8. However, sealings to parents may be performed for children who were not born in the covenant or did not receive that ordinance in life (see 18.1)."

Returning to then Elder Joseph Fielding Smith, he states: "On other occasions, also, President Young taught that we should have hope for the resurrection of stillborn children. 'They are all right,' he said, 'and nothing in the way of sealing or ordinances need be done for them.'" [48]

In harmony with this teaching, the Prophet Joseph Smith declared: "All your losses will be made up to you in the resurrection [of the dead], provided you continue faithful [in mortality]. By the visions of the Almighty I have seen it." [49]

From these enlightening teachings, worthy parents can trust in the Lord to reward them for their sacrifices and trials experienced in mortality, especially with the death of little children. This joyous statement provides assurance and hope: *"And not one hair, neither mote [a small particle], shall be lost, for it is the workmanship of mine [the Lord's] hand"* (Doctrine and Covenants 29:25. Italics added).

Death Of Young People

FROM THE TIME OF ADAM TO THE PRESENT DAY, myriads of young people have passed away. There are numerous reasons for this early demise—the list is very long and very descriptive of explanations.

In conjunction with these realities, Elder Russell M. Nelson wrote: "Regardless of cause, in wartime or peace, when such vigorous and vibrant young men or women have been taken by trauma unforeseen and swift... the grief produced among survivors is sudden and unrelenting."

Continuing, he writes: "While speaking at the funeral of such a young man, the Prophet Joseph Smith also reflected upon the death of his oldest brother, Alvin, and his youngest brother, Don Carlos. He said: 'It has been hard for me to... see these young men upon whom we have leaned for support and comfort taken from us in the midst of their youth. Yes, it has been hard to be reconciled to these things... yet I know we ought to be still and know it is of God, and be reconciled to His will; all is right.'"[50]

In his own words, Elder Nelson wrote: "But to the parents of a beloved young person who has passed through the gateway, death could loom as a span of sadness, or it could become the gateway to other opportunity unforeseen. Parents meet the challenge in various ways." [51]

What of good parents who have disobedient or wayward youth? These youth are no longer active in the Church and rebel against gospel standards that were taught at home and at church. In addition, good parents have adult children—including returned missionaries—who purposely choose to be inactive and live a life that is not in harmony with the teachings of The Church of Jesus Christ of Latter-day Saints.

Regarding these realities, Elder Nelson said: "When those deeds result in disobedience or demise, their parents and loved ones need special consoling." [52]

Speaking to parents of wayward children, Elder Orson F. Whitney's Conference address in April 1929 gives assurance and hope: "The prophet Joseph Smith declared—and he never taught more comforting doctrine—that the eternal sealings [performed in temples] of faithful parents and the divine promises made to them for valiant service in the Cause of Truth, would save not only themselves but likewise their posterity. Though some of the sheep may wander, the eye of the Shepherd is upon them and sooner or later they will feel the tentacles of Divine Providence reaching out after them, and drawing them back to the fold. Either in this life or in the life to come, they will return. They will have to pay their debt to justice; they will suffer for their sins; and may tread a thorny path, but if it leads them at last, like the penitent prodigal, to a loving and forgiving Father's heart and home, the painful experience will not have been in vain. Pray for your careless and disobedient children; hold on to them with your faith. Hope on, trust on, till you see the salvation of God.

"Who are these straying sheep—these wayward sons and daughters? They are children of the Covenant, heirs to the promise, and have received, if baptized, the Gift of the Holy Ghost, which makes manifest the things of God." [53]

With a promise, Elder Nelson wrote: "Our young sons and daughters—precious youth of the noble birthright—if called through the gateway by whatever cause, will yet participate in the glorious gifts provided by the Atonement of Jesus Christ." [54]

Death Of Adults

"THE VAST MAJORITY OF US WILL EXPERIENCE THE joys and the aches that accompany a full span of life. Our passing will come when we are mature or even aged adults. We will also (if we haven't done so already) part company with parents after one or both of them have reached the so-called golden age." [55]

My grandparents and parents have passed away. Each was genuinely cherished and loved. My mother was in her ninety-second year at the time of her death. My father was two days short of ninety-four. Even though each was advanced in age, my sister and I were reluctant to say good-bye.

Though the following personal experiences are not unique, they have greatly broadened my understanding of death and the glorious promises that temple covenants will unite families eternally.

A year after my mission, I married my beautiful bride, Janice Smith, in the Salt Lake Temple. Three beautiful daughters were born of this union. Due to a rare disease of the pumping muscle of the heart, Janice passed away on my oldest daughter's fourth birthday. She was only twenty-two years of age.

I was fortunate to marry my beautiful bride, Susan Conlin, in the Ogden Temple. Three beautiful daughters were born of this union. This marriage ended in divorce (she has passed away since).

I was blessed to marry my beautiful bride, Brenda Lamb, in the Logan Temple. I adopted her handsome young son, and through our union, we had a handsome son. After forty-one years of marriage, Brenda unexpectedly passed away in her sleep.

Returning to my first wife, Janice, then Doctor Russell M. Nelson consulted with Doctor Richard White, Janice's cardiologist, and Doctor Nelson visited me and family members regarding Janice's heart disease. Several years later, I wrote a letter thanking then Elder Russell M. Nelson for his great assistance and visit. In his letter to me, he wrote (due to the passing of his wife): "Thank you for reminding me of my visit with you and your family. You have endured one of the most difficult trials a man can have in this life, after the passing of a beloved companion." [56]

How true this is. Not only have I experienced this once, but twice! For me, the passing of time has softened the void of not having association and conversations with a beloved companion in mortality! In addition, through Temple covenants performed in temples, and by remaining faithful until the end of my mortal life, I will be united with these beautiful eternal companions. (Admittedly, I'm a little nervous about how this family dynamic will work, but I have trust in the Lord that He will help each to love and care for one another.)

It is written: "For whom the Lord loveth he chasteneth" (Hebrews 12:6). Because of this scripture, and my own experience with the demise of beloved wives, I have half-seriously and half-wittingly said out loud: "Thank you! Now, go love someone else."

Speaking from experience and observation, Elder Nelson has truthfully written about chastening: "So it is with prophets past, present, and future. They too 'must be chastened and tried, even as Abraham (D&C 101:4).'" Continuing, he writes: "An expression of the Lord is even more explicit: 'After much tribulation come the blessings (D&C 58:4).'"

"Many people in the twilight of life are compelled to tolerate long and difficult days. They have firsthand knowledge of the oft-repeated divine injunction to 'endure to the end.' One of those scriptures may serve to sample the many. The Savior said, 'Be patient in afflictions, for thou shalt have many; but endure them, for, lo, I am with thee, even unto the end of thy days (D&C 24:8.).' The promise of such celestial companionship [and association with loved ones] is most reassuring." [57]

He has also truthfully written: "Finally, to the adult, to the aged and the disabled, the gateway of death may lead to welcome release from the infirmities of physical imprisonment. [And this] gateway opens the opportunities newly born. Well worth the working and the waiting are the possibilities of heavenly homecoming, family reunion, resurrection, immortality, and eternal life." [58]

The Veil Is Sometimes Thin

THERE ARE DIFFERENT MEANINGS FOR THE WORD *veil*. For members of The Church of Jesus Christ, there are three distinct meanings: (1) When we are born in mortality, a veil of forgetfulness is placed over our minds, so we do not remember living with our Heavenly Father in the premortal existence. (2) There is a linen veil in each LDS temple, symbolic of our Savior, Jesus Christ. (3) When we experience a mortal death, we pass through an unseen veil and enter a peaceful place called the spirit world.

Regarding the first and third meaning of the word *veil*, President Ezra Taft Benson, thirteenth President of the Church, told how righteous people would feel when they die and pass through the veil: "We once knew well our Elder Brother and His and our Father in Heaven. We rejoiced at the prospects of earth life that could make it possible for us to have a fullness of joy. We could hardly wait to demonstrate to our Father and our Brother, the Lord, how much we loved them and how we would be obedient to them in spite of the earthly opposition of the evil one.

"Now we are here [in mortality]. *Our memories are veiled*. We are showing God and ourselves what we can do. [Note these words:] *Nothing is going to startle us more when we pass through the veil to the other side than to realize how well we know our Father and how familiar His face is to us...* what life and sacrifice we can daily, hourly, instantly make for God. If we give our all, we will get His all from the greatest of all." [59]

Though there are several examples that the veil is sometimes thin, for this work, a small number of these experiences will be presented. We begin with what has been described as the First Vision.

At age fourteen, Joseph Smith was the first person in this final dispensation of times to have the veil temporarily removed in mortality. In the spring of 1820, Joseph entered the woods near his family farm and "kneeled down and began to offer up the desires of [his] heart to God." This young lad says, "I had scarcely done so, when immediately I was seized upon by some power which entirely overcame me, and had such an astonishing influence over me as to bind my tongue so that I could not speak. Thick darkness gathered around me, and it seemed to me for a time as if I were doomed to sudden destruction. But, exerting all my powers to call upon God to deliver me out of the power of this enemy which had seized upon me, and at the very moment when I was ready to sink into despair and abandon myself to destruction—not to an imaginary ruin, but to the power of some actual being from the unseen world, who had such marvelous power as I had never before felt in any being."

The Prophet states that "just at this moment of great alarm, I saw a pillar of light exactly over my head, above the brightness of the sun, which descended gradually until it fell upon me. It no sooner appeared than I found myself delivered from the enemy which held me bound. When the light rested upon me I saw two Personages, whose brightness and glory defy all description, standing above me in the air. One of them spake unto me, *calling me by name* and said, pointing to the other—This is My Beloved Son. Hear Him! I asked the Personages who stood above me in the light, which of all the sects was right (for at this time it had never entered into my heart that all were wrong)—and which I should join. I was answered that I must join none of them... and many other things did he say unto me, which I cannot write at this time." (Joseph Smith—History 1:3-20).

Millions of people worldwide, including this author, have received a testimony of the truthfulness of this glorious vision by the power of the Holy Ghost and that both God the Father and His Beloved Son knew Joseph Smith, for he was called by name. This vision completely verifies that the unseen veil between mortality and the spirit world is sometimes thin.

We continue with additional experiences, without commentary.

MORONI'S VISIT

The Prophet Joseph Smith's own words about the coming forth of the Book of Mormon: "On the evening of the... twenty-first of September [1823]... I betook myself to prayer and supplication to Almighty God... While I was thus in the act of calling upon God, I discovered a light appearing in my room... when immediately a personage appeared at my bedside, standing in the air, for his feet did not touch the floor. He had on a loose robe of most exquisite whiteness... I could discover that he had no other clothing on but this robe, as it was open, so that I could see into his bosom.

"Not only was his robe exceedingly white, but his whole person was glorious beyond description, and his countenance was like lightning... *He called me by name,* and said unto me that he was a messenger sent from the presence of God to me, and that his name was Moroni; that God had a work for me to do... He said there was a book deposited, written upon gold plates, giving an account of the former inhabitants of this continent, and the source from whence they sprang. He also said that the fulness of the everlasting Gospel was contained in it, as delivered by the Savior to the ancient inhabitants..." (Joseph Smith—History 1:29-34. Italics added).

<u>VISION OF THE CELESTIAL KINGDOM</u>

"On the twenty-first day of January, 1836, the First Presidency, and a number of the presiding brethren in the Church, assembled in the Kirtland Temple where they engaged in the ordinances of the endowment, as far as it had at that time been revealed... Following this ordinance the following vision and revelation were given the Prophet, making known to him and through him to the Church one of the most important principles pertaining to the salvation of men.

"The heavens were opened upon us, and I beheld the celestial kingdom of God, and the glory thereof... I saw Father Adam and Abraham, and my father and my mother, *my brother Alvin, that has long since slept,* and marveled how it was that he obtained an inheritance in that kingdom, seeing that he had departed this life before the Lord had set his hand to gather Israel the second time, *and had not been baptized for the remission of sins.*

Giving comfort and knowledge to the Prophet, the Lord said:

"*All who have died without a knowledge of this Gospel, who would have received it if they had been permitted to tarry, shall be heirs of the celestial kingdom of God;* also all that shall die henceforth without a knowledge of it, who would have received it with all their hearts, shall be heirs of that kingdom, for I, the Lord, will judge all men according to their works, according to the desires of their hearts..." [60]

<u>FUNERAL OF PRESIDENT JEDEDIAH M. GRANT</u>

In an earlier section, it was explained that President Heber C. Kimball visited with President Jedediah M. Grant, who was ill.

At Grant's funeral, President Kimball related

the following: "Brother Heber, I have been into the spirit world two nights in succession, and, of all the dreads that ever came across me, *the worst was to have to again return to my body, though I had to do it.* But O, says he, the order and government that were there! When in the spirit world, I saw the order of righteous men and women; beheld them organized in their several grades, and there appeared to be no obstruction to my vision ... I looked to see whether there was any disorder there, but there was none; neither could I see any death nor any darkness, disorder, or confusion. He said that the people he there saw were organized into family capacities; and when he looked at them, he saw grade after grade, and all were organized and in perfect harmony. He would mention one item after another and say, 'Why, it is just as brother Brigham says it is; it is just as he has told us many a time'…

"He saw his wife; she was the first person that came to him...he said that she looked beautiful and had their little child, that died on the Plains, in her arms, and said, 'Mr. Grant, here is little Margaret; you know that the wolves ate her up, but it did not hurt her; here she is alright.'

"…He asked his wife Caroline where Joseph and Hyrum and Father Smith and others were; she replied, 'they have gone away ahead to perform and transact business for us.'

"…He also spoke of the buildings he saw there, remarking that the Lord gave Solomon wisdom and poured gold and silver into his hands that he might display his skill and ability, and said that the temple erected by Solomon was much inferior to the most ordinary buildings he saw in the spirit world.

"In regard to gardens, says brother Grant, 'I have seen good gardens on this earth, but I never saw any to compare with those that were there. I saw flowers of numerous kinds, and some with from fifty to a hundred different colored flowers growing upon one stalk'

"…After mentioning the things that he had seen, *he [again] spoke of how much he disliked to return and resume his body*, after having seen the beauty and glory of the spirit world, where the righteous spirits are gathered together." [61]

<u>ELLA JENSEN</u>

The following story is told from two sources. The first is recorded by Francis M. Gibbons: "It was March 3, 1891, and for several long weeks Ella Jensen, a young girl of 19 at Brigham City, Utah, had lingered, almost between life and death, with scarlet fever. Leah Rees…was serving her as night nurse, and it was about three or four o'clock in the morning when, as Leah reports it, 'I was suddenly awakened by Ella calling me to get the comb, brush, and scissors. She explained that she wanted to brush her hair and trim her fingernails and get all ready, 'For,' she said, 'they are coming to get me at ten o'clock this morning.'

"'I asked who was coming to get her,'

"'Uncle Hans Jensen and the messengers,' she replied. 'I am going to die, and they are coming at ten o' clock to get me and take me away.'

"'I tried to quiet her, saying that she would feel better in the morning if she would try to sleep.'

"'No,' she said, 'I am not going to sleep anymore, but I am going to spend all the time getting ready.'

"'. . . As I was brushing her hair, she asked me to call her parents.'

"The parents were called, and as they entered the room, the daughter told them that her Uncle Hans, who was dead, had suddenly appeared in the room, while she was awake with her eyes open, and told her that messengers would be there at ten o' clock to conduct her into the spirit world. The father and mother feared that the girl was delirious and tried to get her quiet and go to sleep.

"She knew their thoughts and said, 'I know what I am talking about. No, I am not going to sleep anymore. I know I am going to die, and that they are coming to get me.'" [62]

The second information is recorded by Leroi C. Snow: "At about eight o'clock...the father and mother remained at the bedside. Relatives and friends who had heard of Ella's sudden relapse came to see her.

"Towards ten o' clock... Jake, the father, who was holding his daughter's hand, felt the pulse become very weak. A few moments later he turned to his wife saying: 'Althea, she is dead'... The heart-broken parents wept and grieved at the loss of their beautiful daughter." [63]

Returning to Francis M. Gibbons' description: "Ella's father left at once to report to President [Lorenzo] Snow [who was President of the Quorum of the Twelve Apostles] and consult [with] him regarding arrangements for the funeral. Sister Nelson washed and laid Ella out, dressed her in clean linen, and Budd took the doctor back home, who had been called in this emergency. Meanwhile, news of her death spread about. It was towards noon when Jacob Jensen, Ella's father, reported to President Snow at the tabernacle service, because it was more than a mile to town and he had to hitch up the horse to drive there. They returned together with Rudger Clawson, who was then the President of the Box Elder Stake.

"After standing at Ella's bedside for a minute or two, President Snow asked if there were any consecrated oil in the house. All were greatly surprised, but the oil was secured for him. He handed the bottle of oil to Brother Clawson and asked him to anoint Ella, after which Brother Snow confirmed the anointing.

"Particularly impressive, among others, were these words that he used, 'Dear Ella, I command you, in the name of the Lord Jesus Christ, to come back and live. Your mission is not ended.' His voice was very commanding, 'Come back, Ella, come back! Your work upon the earth is not yet completed. Come back! You shall yet live to perform a great mission.'

"Ella remained in her dead condition for more than an hour after President Snow administered to her, or more than three hours in all after she had died. Her mother and father were sitting there watching by the bedside, when all at once she opened her eyes, looked about the room, and saw them sitting there. But she still looked for someone else, and the first thing she said was, 'Where is he? Where is he?'

"'Where is who?'

"'Why, Brother Snow,' she replied. 'He called me back.' They explained to her that Brother Snow and Brother Clawson were very busy and could not remain, and that they had gone. Ella then dropped her head back on her pillow, saying,

'Why did he call me back? I was so happy and did not want to come back.'

"Then Ella Jensen began to relate her marvelous experiences; marvelous both as to the incidents themselves, and as to the great number of them that occurred in the short space of time between three and four hours. And furthermore, the very nature of these incidents prove that she was telling nothing but the truth.

"'At ten o'clock my spirit left my body,' related Ella. 'It took me some time to make up my mind to go, as I could hear and see the folks crying and mourning over me. It was very hard to me to leave them, but as soon as I had a glimpse of the other world, I was anxious to go, and all the care and worry left me.

"'I entered a large hall. It was so long that I could not see the end of it. It was filled with people. As I was conducted through the throng, the first person I recognized was my Grandpa H. P. Jensen, who was sitting in one end of the room writing. He looked up and seemed surprised to see me. He said, 'Why! There is my granddaughter, Ella!'

"'He was very much pleased, greeted me, and as he continued with his writing, I passed on through the room and met a great many of my relatives and friends. It was like going along the crowded street of a large city where you meet many people, only a very few of whom you recognize.

"'Some seemed to be in family groups. As there were only a few whom I could recognize and who knew me, I kept moving on. Some inquired about their friends and relatives on the earth. Among the number was my cousin. He asked me how the folks were getting along and said it grieved him to hear that some of the boys were using tobacco, liquor, and many things that were injurious to them.

"'This proved to me that the people in the other world know to a great extent what happens here on the earth. The people were all dressed in white or cream...Everybody appeared to be perfectly happy. I was having a very pleasant visit with each one that I knew. Finally, I reached the end of that long room. I opened a door and went into another room filled with children. They were all arranged in perfect order, the largest ones in the back rows all around the room. They seemed to be convened in a sort of Primary or Sunday School, which was presided over by Aunt Eliza R. Snow. There were hundreds of small children there.'

"'It was,' continued Ella, 'while I was standing listening to the children singing, 'Gladly Meeting, Kindly Greeting,' that I heard President Lorenzo Snow call me. He said, 'Sister Ella, you must come back, as your mission is not yet finished here on earth.' So I just spoke to Aunt Eliza R. Snow and told her that I must go back.

"'Returning through the large room, I told the people I was going back to the earth, but they seemed to want me to stay with them. I obeyed the call, although it was very much against my desire, as such perfect peace and happiness prevailed there–no suffering and no sorrow. I was so taken up with all I saw and heard that I did hate very much to leave that beautiful place.'

"This has always been a source of comfort to me. I learned by this experience that we should not grieve too much for our departed loved ones, and especially at the time they leave us. I think we should be just as calm and quiet as possible, because, as I was leaving my mortal life, the only regret I had was that the folks were grieving so much for me. But I soon forgot all about this world in my delight with the other. For more than three hours my spirit was gone from my body. As I returned, I could see my body lying on the bed and the folks gathered about in the room. I wanted to stay only a short time on earth to comfort them.

"Ella frequently told of the terrible suffering that she experienced when the spirit again entered the body. There was practically no pain on leaving the body in death, but the intense pain was almost unbearable in coming back to life. Not only this, but for months, and even years afterward, she experienced new aches and pains and physical disorders that she had never known before. Some of the people Ella described as having met in this spirit sojourn were her aunts and second cousins, long since dead and laid away before she was born. She told her Aunt Harriet Wight, who had lost two daughters, not to mourn them, for she had seen them and had talked with them, and they were very happy in their new sphere of existence.

"Many relatives and others visited Ella, and she told them the same story—of how she had met their relatives and friends over there, how happy they were, and that they had asked about their loved ones here. When Leah Rees, her night nurse, came to stay with Ella the next night, she told her about having seen her (Leah's) father and several others of her people who had passed away, as well as her own Grandpa Jensen–all of whom appeared very happy.'

"One person Ella was puzzled about seeing in the spirit world was little Alphie, the son of Alphonzo H. Snow. He had been in her Sunday School class in the First Ward, and she did not know that he had just died. When she told her mother, she said, 'Yes, Ella, little Alphie is dead, too. He died early this morning while you were so very sick. We knew you loved him and that it would be a shock to you, so we did not tell you about his death.' But, nevertheless, she had recognized the little fellow happily singing among the children under the direction of Eliza R. Snow."

As the reader will remember, in an earlier section, President Joseph F. Smith declared: "If you see one of your children that has passed away it may appear to you in the form in which you would recognize it, the form of childhood." [64] From this statement, it is this author's view that Ella was able to see hundreds of small children, particularly little Alphie, because she was able to recognize them in the form of childhood.

Returning to the story, Ella continued:

"'It was while sitting there listening to those children that she heard a voice coming to her in commanding tones, apparently from a long distance, which said, 'Come back, Ella, come back! Your work on earth is not yet completed.' And, although she had no desire to come back, but on the contrary, felt determined to remain in that beautiful world, the voice was so authoritative in manner that it seemed to draw, yes, actually draw her spirit out of that room and back to her body. She felt compelled to follow it and return to earth, where she filled to the fullness, her life's mission on earth, becoming a mother in Israel, and doing much for the glory of God and her own exaltation in the service of the Lord. She is now known as Mrs. Henry Wight of Brigham City, Utah...[and] gave birth to eight children, and lived to the age of eighty-six." [65]

<u>ELDER JAMES E. FAUST</u>

We now turn our attention to then-Elder James E. Faust, who was an Assistant to the Twelve Apostles and later was set apart as a member of the First Presidency:

"My wife's mother's twin sister died a few weeks ago and a few days before she passed away, she came down [from upstairs] to breakfast and told her family, she being quite aged, that, 'You're not going to believe this, but last night Jim [meaning her brother Jim Hamilton, former bishop out in Lincoln Ward and the patriarch of the Granite Stake until last year when he passed away] came to me last night and told me that my time was coming, *that he'd be back for me in just a few days and that I should get ready* and tell you all. And then she said that mother was lonesome and missed her daughters,' and then made a very significant statement. She said that 'Bishop Hamilton said the people on the other side [in the world of spirits], some of them have a hard time to listen to the message of the gospel.'" [66]

Elder Russell M. Nelson explains: "No doubt many of us are aware of additional accounts of communication from the deceased to friends or family members living here in mortality. While the validity of such accounts may not always be easy to ascertain, there can be little doubt that our loved ones are near in spirit…[accordingly,] we are separated only by the thin veil draped from the gateway [of death in mortality]." [67]

Choice Of Living

Regarding agency—which is the freedom to choose between right or wrong—the Old Testament Prophet, Moses, was told this truth: "Satan rebelled against me, and sought to destroy the agency of man, which I, the Lord God had given him." (Moses 4:3). Moses was further told: "It is given unto [thy children] to know good from evil; wherefore they are agents unto themselves." (Moses 6:56).

Elder Nelson also explains: "Many people opt to append the adjective *free* to describe agency. But the expression 'free agency' is not scriptural terminology. Scripture refers only to 'moral agency.' [Note these words:] The Lord said that 'every man [or woman] may act in doctrine and principle pertaining to futurity [time in the future], according to the *moral agency* which I have given unto him, that every man [or woman] may be accountable for his [or her] own sins in the day of judgement." (D&C 101:78. Italics added).

Continuing, he states: "Moral agency goes hand in hand with moral accountability. Decisions of a moral nature are based on faith in the Lord, the giver of moral law. The Word of Wisdom is part of that divine code of moral law. It is spiritual in nature. Obedience to it carries physical reward as well." [68]

FAITH TO BE HEALED

When an individual is not feeling well, or is about to die, and asks for a priesthood blessing, the Lord gave this instruction: "He that hath faith in me to be healed, and is not appointed unto death, shall be healed" (Doctrine and Covenants 42:48). Regarding this scripture, then Elder Spencer W. Kimball, of the Quorum of the Twelve Apostles, said: "If one is not 'appointed unto death' and if sufficient faith is developed, life can be spared. But if there is not enough faith, many die before their time. [Note these words:] It is evident that even the righteous will not always be healed, and even those of great faith will die when it is according to the purposes of God. Joseph Smith died in his thirties as did the Savior. Solemn prayers were answered negatively." [69]

<u>RESPECTING OUR BODIES</u>

Elder Nelson wrote: "Faithful men and women respect their bodies as holy temples with proper nutrition and care, appropriate exercise, rest as the Lord has recommended, chastity, and moral fidelity. Longevity is likewise enhanced for those who choose to honor their parents." [70]

Suicide

A VAST AMOUNT OF PEOPLE KNOW OF A FAMILY member or friend who has died by suicide. In the view of this author, it seems that this premature death is becoming more prevalent. Some of the following factors have greatly increased the reality of teenagers dying by suicide, with no specific order: (1) Being bullied at school or through chat lines on the Internet; (2) Repeated child abuse, either mentally, physically, or sexually; (3) Strong influences to change gender identity. While transitioning, the drugs taken greatly affect hormone levels, which can greatly increase anxiety and depression; (4) TikTok and other social media glamorizing dangerous acts or stunts, which has caused several deaths; (5) Sexting or sextortion. To give one example only: A young man received an Instagram message from a pretty girl his age, who he had never met. After a couple of flirty messages, each agreed to exchange intimate photos. Immediately after sending, the pleasant conversations changed. The criminals behind the account threatened to release the images, demanding money. This young man sent these predators from $300 to $600. After that amount was paid, these evil men asked for more money. Being greatly shamed and depressed, this young man felt that the only way out of this situation was death by suicide; (6) Taking unprescribed Fentanyl, which instantaneously causes death, or taking harmful drugs which can greatly enhance suicidal thoughts; and (7) Being deeply depressed and not seeking medical or professional help greatly enhances a person committing death by suicide. The list could continue.

Though we don't know the reason, we truly need to show compassion and love to those who have been affected by this event.

Elder Nelson wisely explained: "Perhaps no topic touches on the importance of choice in longevity as directly as does that of suicide. The act of taking one's own life is truly a tragedy because it creates so many victims. Family and countless friends are left to bear feelings of underserved misery and guilt…Unfortunately, forces of stress and depression incite behavior that is not always rational." [71]

With compassion and an acknowledgement, Elder Bruce R. McConkie wrote: "Persons subject to great stresses may lose control of themselves and become mentally clouded to the point that they are no longer accountable for their acts. Such are not to be condemned for taking their own lives. It should also be remembered that judgment is the Lord's; he knows the thoughts, intents, and abilities of men [and women]; and he in his infinite wisdom will make all things right in due course." [72]

The following story was related by a friend:

"My wife and I met with a less active sister in our ward who stated that she had attempted suicide several years ago, and the feeling came to her in that time of extreme stress that this was the absolutely right thing to do. It was only through the timely discovery of her incapacitation [incapable of natural or normal functioning] by a family member that she was saved. 'Truly, Satan can appear, act and sound like a being of light!'"

In support of this quoted statement, Paul said that *"Satan himself is [at times] transformed into an angel of light..."* (2 Corinthians 11:14. Italics added). In addition, "Korihor was one person to whom such an appearance was made. After being struck dumb by the power of God, he wrote this confession: 'Behold, *the devil hath deceived me; for he appeared unto me in the form of an angel*, and said unto me: Go and reclaim this people, for they have all gone astray after an unknown God...and he taught me that which I should say... *because they were pleasing unto the carnal mind...*" (Alma 30:53. Italics added). [73]

Using scriptures, Elder McConkie skillfully explains these doctrines: "Following the pre-existent choosing of Christ and the rejecting of Lucifer to be the Redeemer in the great plan of salvation, *Satan and one-third of the spirit hosts ... came out in open rebellion against the Father...* (Moses 4:1-4; Abra. 3:24-28; D&C 29:36-38) [and] is called by John the war in heaven (Rev.12:4-9). The same inspired writer then goes on to explain that after Satan was cast out onto the earth, he was given power 'to make war with the saints, and to overcome them.' (Rev. 12; 13). The warfare of the saints on earth (Eph. 6:10-18; 2 Tim. 4:7-8) is a continuation of the war in heaven. It is a war between truth and error, between light and darkness...between Christ and Satan." [74]

With these truths established, we turn to the revealing words of President George Q. Cannon, a counselor in the First Presidency. He said:

"Will you be true and loyal to God with the curtain [veil] drawn between you and Him, shut out from His presence, and in the midst of darkness and temptation, *with Satan and his invisible hosts all around you*, bringing all manner of evil influences to bear upon you?…We are left to be governed by the influences that we invite, *and there are any number of evil influences around us, whispering into our ears and hearts all manner of [bad or evil] things…*" [75]

We now return to the story my friend told me of a sister in his ward who stated that several years ago she had attempted suicide, *and the feeling came to her in that time of extreme stress that this was the absolutely right thing to do.* From what President Cannon said, it is this author's view that it is possible this feeling came from the whispering of Satan or one his invisible followers, and that many individuals—particularly teenagers—have the compelling feeling that his or her demise is absolutely the right thing to do.

With this stated, we read the inspired words of Elder Russell M. Ballard, of the Quorum of the Twelve Apostles, who studied the topic of suicide extensively and made these observations: "I feel that judgment for sin is not always as cut-and-dried as some of us seem to think. The Lord said, 'Thou shall not kill.' [He then asks a series of questions:] Does that mean that every person who kills will be condemned, no matter the circumstances? … I feel that the Lord also recognizes differences in intent and circumstances: Was the person who took his life mentally ill? Was he or she so deeply depressed as to be unbalanced or otherwise emotionally disturbed? Was the suicide a tragic, pitiful call for help that went unheeded too long or progressed faster than the victim intended? Did he or she somehow not understand the seriousness of the act? Was he or she suffering from a chemical imbalance that led to despair and loss of self-control?"

He then states this truth: "Obviously, we do not know the full circumstances surrounding every suicide. Only the Lord knows all the details, and he it is who will judge our actions on earth. When he does judge us, I feel he will take all things into consideration: our genetic and chemical makeup, our mental state, our intellectual capacity, the teachings we have received, the traditions of our fathers, our health, and so forth...Thus, a person who has never heard of the Word of Wisdom, for example, and who becomes an alcoholic will be judged differently from one who knows the Word of Wisdom, and understands it, and then chooses the course that leads to alcoholism..."

With faith and hope, he stated: "I draw an important conclusion from the words of the Prophet [Joseph Smith]: Suicide is a sin—a very grievous one, yet the Lord will not judge the person who commits that sin strictly by the act itself. The Lord will look at that person's circumstances and the degree of his accountability at the time of the act." [76]

In the grand vision of the redemption of the dead, President Joseph F. Smith, sixth President of the Church, declared: "The dead who repent will be redeemed, through the obedience to the ordinances of the house of God [temples]. And, after they have paid the penalty of their transgressions, and are washed clean, shall receive a reward according to their works, for they are heirs of salvation." (Doctrine and Covenants 138:58-59). Through the marvelous atonement of Jesus Christ, teenagers who have died by suicide, have great hope for progression in the spirit world, if they truly "repent" and the required "ordinances" are performed by proxy in a temple, for they are "heirs of salvation."

In harmony with this teaching, Elder Russell M. Nelson has written: "Suicide is a choice—a grievous choice—that abbreviates longevity. Its victims include those who suffer because of that choice. They need and deserve the reassurance of the gospel and the knowledge that life for their loved one continues.

Immortality of the soul applies to all, as does the privilege of repentance and [of] forgiveness." [77]

Now, on a related subject, in the Gospel Library of The Church of Jesus Christ of Latter-day Saints, Elder Dale G. Renlund, of the Quorum of the

Twelve Apostles, has spoken well regarding various aspects of suicide through seven short videos, lasting from one to three minutes, dated July 2018.

"WHAT ABOUT EUTHANASIA?"

As a renowned heart doctor and as a member of the Quorum of the Twelve Apostles, Elder Russell M. Nelson wrote these declarative words: "In recent times, the topic of euthanasia, or mercy killing, has received increasing public attention. *I mention it here only to condemn it*…Merciful as it may seem superficially, the choice to take an innocent life cannot be reposed with any person or panel of specialists."

Further, "No human can qualify to take [life] away under the guise of pity or piety. Society must not create a board of 'expert exterminators.' [Note these words:] Medical knowledge should help the sick to endure to the end, but never to create that end." [78]

"PROLONGATION OF LIFE BY MEDICAL MEANS"

In speaking about choices when an individual is nearing the end of his or her mortal life, Elder Nelson stated: "We live in a modern medical era of sophisticated life-support systems, intensive-care units, and expert physicians skilled in the care of those who are critically ill...[speaking as a doctor, he wrote:] In my many years of experience caring for those who are critically ill, this question of prolongation of life was usually resolved without much anguish. Quiet and calm conversations between physicians and families were very helpful...Consultation with the Lord in prayer is a vital part of all important decision making. Those who are able to attend the temple will find the House of the Lord to be a sacred setting in which such matters may be prayerfully pondered. Counsel with members of the family, local church leaders, or trusted friends is very helpful...Large as those decisions may loom at the moment, the consequences are less time-sensitive when viewed from an eternal perspective. [Note these words:] *More important than the length of life is the quality of life.* And more important than worldly accomplishments is fidelity to God, family, and country...More... families are providing opportunity for their loved one who is terminally ill to pass through life's exit gateway in comfortable surroundings at home. These choices are shaped to the individual circumstances. They pertain to propriety as well as longevity." [79]

<u>SALVATION FOR THE DEAD</u>

It is the design, purpose, and work of God the Father to bring to pass the immortality and eternal life of mankind (Moses 1:39). As has been explained, all mankind will experience death. Though death can be very difficult to understand, there is a glorious path the Savior provided to overcome it. We will spend the remainder of this work reviewing doctrines related to priesthood, and significant events that transpired before and after the death and resurrection of Jesus Christ, and how all mankind will be resurrected and gain eternal life and immortality.

Priesthood

IN THIS SECTION, WE WILL TURN OUR ATTENTION to a very important doctrine of The Church of Jesus Christ of Latter-day Saints—priesthood.

Condensing information from the sermons and writings of President Joseph F. Smith, sixth president of the Church, Elder Bruce R. McConkie explains that "priesthood is the power and authority of God delegated to man on earth to act in all things for the salvation of men [mankind]. It is the power by which the gospel is preached; by which the ordinances of salvation are performed so that they will be binding on earth and in heaven; by which men are sealed up unto eternal life, being assured of the fulness of the Father's kingdom hereafter; and by which in due course the Lord will govern the nations of the earth and all that pertains to them (*Gospel Doctrine*, 5th ed., pp. 136-200)." [80]

Continuing, Elder McConkie wrote: "Thus the Prophet [Joseph Smith] taught: '*All priesthood is Melchizedek, but there are different portions or degrees of it*' (*Teachings*, p. 180)." Further: "It is, however, proper and common to speak of the two great orders of the priesthood as priesthoods; hence, the revealed statement, 'There are, in the church, two priesthoods, namely, *the Melchizedek and Aaronic, including the Levitical Priesthood.*' (D. & C. 107:1; *Doctrines of Salvation*, vol. 3, pp. 80-183)." [81]

Our Savior, Jesus Christ, taught the Prophet Joseph Smith why the higher priesthood is called Melchizedek Priesthood, "is because Melchizedek was such a great high priest. Before his day [about 2000 B.C.] it was called the Holy Priesthood, after the Order of the Son of God. But out of respect or reverence to the name of the Supreme Being, to avoid the too frequent repetition of his name, they, the church, in ancient days, called that priesthood after Melchizedek, or the Melchizedek Priesthood" (Doctrine and Covenants 107:2-4).

Mount Of Transfiguration

With these truths stated, we now turn to a glorious event which transpired during the mortal life of Jesus. "Approximately one week after Peter's great confession to the Lord that 'thou art the Christ, the Son of the living God' and of Jesus' promise that the keys of the kingdom would be given (Matthew 16:16), *the Master took Peter, James, and John to a high mountain to pray* (Luke 9:28. Italics added)." [82]

As to the time that this transpired: "It was the fall of the year, a time when the Feast of the Tabernacles was celebrated among the Jews. It was half a year before Passover, six months before the Redeemer would be crucified and resurrected." [83]

Though this mountain is not named in the scriptural record, it is believed that it is "Mount

Hermon, north of Caesarea Philippi." In support of this, it is written that "Jesus and his party are known to have been near Caesarea Philippi the week before, and Mark expressly says they did not return to Galilee until after the Transfiguration (Mark 9:30)." [84]

It is noted that Jesus singled *Peter, James, and John* from the rest of the nine Apostles to go to the mountain to pray. The question has been asked: "Why always these three and not various ones or even all of the Twelve?" Answering his own question, Elder McConkie wrote these truth-filled words: "The plain fact is that Peter, James, and John *were the First Presidency of the Church in their day.*" Providing further information, he wrote: "From the fragmentary New Testament accounts we have no way of knowing whether they served as a quorum distinct from the Twelve or whether they continued to serve both in the Presidency and in the Twelve. *But by latter-day revelation we know that they held and restored 'the keys of the kingdom, which belong always unto the Presidency of the High Priesthood'* (D&C 81:2)." [85]

Taking on the role of First Presidency—to lead the Church following the crucifixion of the Mortal Messiah in six months—Peter, James, and John were there to experience marvelous additional training in this sacred place referred to as the Mount of Transfiguration.

While walking up the mountain, these chosen three "asked [Jesus] many questions concerning his sayings." (Joseph Smith Translation Mark 9:1-2). It was late in the evening when they arrived at a solitary place where they would not be disturbed, for Luke explains that Jesus prayed and Peter, James, and John "were heavy with sleep" (Luke 9:32).

"At the proper time the three chief apostles—the First Presidency of the Church—awoke; the time for the participation in the two-realm wonders of that night was at hand." [86] Throughout his *The Mortal Messiah* series, Elder McConkie quoted Frederic W. Farrar, an author who published his book, *The Life of Christ,* in 1874. [Note the well-written words of Farrar:]

"'It was the evening hour when He [Jesus] ascended, and as He climbed the hill-slope with those three chosen witnesses—'The Sons of Thunder and the Man of Rock'—doubtless a solemn gladness dilated His soul; a sense not only of the heavenly calm which that solitary communion with His Heavenly Father would breathe upon the spirit, but still more than this, a sense that He would be supported for the coming hour by ministrations not of earth, and illuminated with a light which needed no aid from sun or moon or stars. He went up to be prepared for death, and He took His three Apostles with Him that, haply, having seen his glory—the glory of the Only Begotten of the Father, full of grace and truth—their hearts might be fortified, their faith strengthened, to gaze unshaken on the shameful insults and unspeakable humiliation of the cross.

"'There, then, He knelt and prayed, and as He prayed, He was elevated far above the toil and misery of the world which had rejected Him. *He was transfigured before them,* and His countenance shone as the sun, and His garments became white as the dazzling snow-fields about them. He was enwrapped in such...glistering brilliance—His whole presence breathed so divine a radiance— that the light, the snow, the lightning are the only things to which the Evangelist can compare that celestial lustre' (Farrar, pp. 394-95. Italics added)." [87]

Later in his mortal ministry, Peter would testify that these three apostles "were eyewitnesses of his majesty" (2 Peter 1:16). From the scriptural record, it is revealed that when Jesus began to pray on the mountain, "the fashion of his countenance was altered" (Luke 9:29). Mark says that *"he was transfigured before them."* (Joseph Smith Translation Mark 9:1; see also Mark 9:2. Italics added). From the Prophet Joseph Smith it was revealed that Peter, James, and John were themselves *"transfigured before him"* (*Teachings*, p. 158. Italics added).

What does it mean to be *transfigured?* It is a "special change in appearance and nature which is wrought upon a person or thing by the power of God. This divine transformation is from a lower to a higher state; it results in a more exalted, impressive, and glorious condition." Further, "By the power of the Holy Ghost many prophets have been transfigured so as to stand in the presence of God and view the visions of eternity." [88]

"John the Baptist, previously beheaded by Herod, apparently was present." (See Mark 9:4; Joseph Smith Translation Mark 9:3). [89]

"At this point," wrote Elder McConkie, "the angelic witness of the atoning sacrifice having been borne by *Moses and Elijah,* and no doubt by John the Baptist also—the two men from ancient Israel, having retained their physical bodies so they might confer priestly authority upon mortals—these two joined with Jesus in conferring upon Peter, James, and John the keys of the kingdom. Moses conferred the keys of the gathering of Israel, Elijah the keys of the sealing power, so that whatever they bound or loosed on earth would be bound or loosed in heaven. [Note:] Jesus himself gave them all else that they needed to preside over his earthly kingdom; to lead all men [mankind] to eternal salvation in the mansions on high; to send the gospel to the ends of the earth; and to seal men up unto eternal life in the kingdom of his Father." [90]

A valid question can be asked: Why was it necessary for Elijah and Moses to give instructions and restore keys as translated beings? Answering, President Joseph Fielding Smith wrote: "But, one says, the Lord could have waited until after his resurrection, and they [Jesus, Elijah, and Moses] could have done it [restored the keys to Peter, James, and John]. It is quite evident, due to the fact that it did so occur, that it had to be done before; and there was a reason. *There may have been other reasons, but that is one reason why Moses and Elijah did not suffer death in the flesh, like other men do.*" [91]

Another reason is that the presiding authority would have been interrupted from the time of Moses' death to Christ's resurrection.

Returning to the scriptural record, Peter, James, and John each "saw in vision the transfiguration of the earth, that is, they saw it renewed and returned to its paradisiacal state—an event that is to take place at the Second Coming when the millennial era is ushered in (D&C 63:20-21. . .)" [92]

In addition, these three *"received their own endowments* [special spiritual blessings and knowledge given worthy and faithful Latter-day Saints in the temples built for that purpose] on the mountain. (*Doctrines of Salvation*, vol. 2, page,

165)." He further writes, "Peter says that while there, they 'received from God the Father [honor] and glory,' seemingly bearing out this conclusion. It also appears that it was while on the mount that they received the *more sure word of prophecy*, it then being revealed to them *that they* were *sealed up unto eternal life*. (2 Pet. 1:16-19; D&C 131:5. Italics added)." [93]

"Apparently Jesus himself was strengthened and encouraged by *Moses and Elijah* so as to be prepared for the infinite sufferings and agony ahead of him in connection with working out the infinite and eternal atonement (As written in *Jesus the Christ*, p. 373)." [94]

It is sure that these "three chosen apostles were taught in plainness [*by Elijah and Moses*] 'of his death and also his resurrection' (JST Luke 9:31), [and these] "teachings...would be of inestimable value to them in the trying days ahead." [95]

At some time during the night, "Peter, speaking impetuously, as was his nature, said: 'Lord, it is good for us to be here'—and truly it was—'if thou wilt, let us make here three tabernacles; one for thee, and one for Moses, and for Elias [Elijah].'" [96] It is written that these booths or tabernacles were made of wattled boughs—consisting of material for making walls interlaced with twigs or branches.[97]

Then, this grand event transpired: "The

ancient Shekinah, the luminous cloud, the visible manifestation of the Divine Presence;... the Shekinah came down from heaven to shield the face and form of God from his earthbound creations.

"Elohim was there in the cloud. That he was seen by the Son we cannot doubt. Whether our Lord's three companions saw within the veil we do not say. . . All that is preserved for us in the New Testament account is that while Peter yet spake of making the three tabernacles...'behold, a bright cloud overshadowed them: and behold the voice out of the cloud, which said,

'This is my beloved Son, in whom I am well pleased; hear ye him.'

"Thus, once again the Divine Voice—the Father of us all; the one above all others whose right it is to command obedience and invite worship of himself—affirmed the eternal truth that Christ is the Son; that salvation comes by the Son; that all men must honor the Son and believe his words; that the only approved course for all men of all races in all ages is: 'Hear ye Him!'...

"Hearing the Divine Voice, the three disciples fell on their faces 'and were sore afraid.' Thereupon Jesus touched them and in tender solicitude said simply, 'Arise, and be not afraid. They did so, and *when they had looked round about with great astonishment, they saw no man any more, save Jesus only, with themselves. And immediately they* departed."

"As they came down the mountain, Jesus said, 'Tell the vision to no man, until the Son of man be risen again from the dead.' The wonders they had seen could not then lawfully be uttered even to the others of the Twelve, nor could they be understood by any without the enlightening power of the Holy Ghost." [98] [See Matthew 17: 4-9; Joseph Smith Translation Matthew 17:5; Mark 9: 5-9; Joseph Smith Translation Mark 9:6; Luke 9: 33-36; Joseph Smith Translation Luke 9: 33, 36].

"Thereafter the keys were given to all of the Twelve [Apostles]. (Matthew 18:18)... As it was anciently, so it is today. Priesthoods and keys and heavenly powers are just as important as they ever were." [99]

<u>JOHN THE BAPTIST, PETER, JAMES, AND JOHN</u>

Again, from what transpired on this mount, it is this author's view that at an unspecified time, our Savior instructed these four valiant leaders to restore important priesthood keys. Accordingly, "John the Baptist, ministering as *a resurrected and glorified being*, on the 15th day of May in 1829, conferred upon Joseph Smith and Oliver Cowdery the Aaronic Priesthood and all of the keys and power that unto it do appertain. It 'holds the keys of the ministering of angels, and of the gospel of repentance, and of baptism by immersion for the remission of sins.' (D&C 13)...

"Soon thereafter Peter and James, *in resurrected glory*, and John their fellow minister, *serving as a translated being*, came also to Joseph Smith and Oliver Cowdery. These heavenly ministrants conferred upon their mortal fellow the Melchizedek Priesthood, the keys of the kingdom of God, and the keys of the dispensation of the fulness of times (D&C 27:12-13). This higher priesthood embraces within it the holy apostleship and is the power by which the gospel and [The Church of Jesus Christ of Latter-day Saints] are administered, and by which the gift of the Holy Ghost and salvation in its eternal fulness are made available to men [mankind]. Being thus empowered from on high, the recipients of so great a boon were able to organize the church and kingdom of God on earth, which they did on the 6th of April in 1830." [100] More about this occurrence will be given later.

Death And Resurrection Of Jesus

RETURNING TO THE MORTAL MINISTRY OF OUR Savior, it is written that "Jesus was nailed to the cross during the forenoon of that fateful Friday," wrote Elder Talmage, "probably between nine and ten o' clock. At noontide the light of the sun was obscured, and black darkness spread over the whole land. The terrifying gloom continued for a period of three hours. This remarkable phenomenon has received no satisfactory explanation from science...The darkness was brought about by miraculous operation of natural laws directed by divine power." [101] [See Matthew 27:45; Mark 15:33].

We can only imagine what darkness, grief, and

misery must have been their feeling, at least in the view of this author, for those devoted women who were close to the cross in the Savior's final hours.

With a full knowledge that Jesus was no longer forsaken by His Father and God, and that His atoning sacrifice had been accepted, and that His ministry on the earth had been completed, He exclaimed in a loud and triumphal voice, "Father, it is finished, thy will is done." Then, He voluntarily "yielded up the ghost," and He physically died (Joseph Smith Translation Matthew 27:4; See also Luke 23:46).

Regarding the age of Jesus at this time, Farrar wrote this informative view: "It was but for thirty-three short years of a short lifetime that He lived on earth; it was but for three broken and troubled years that He preached the Gospel of the Kingdom." [102]

EVENTS THAT TRANSPIRED

"The death of Christ was accompanied by terrifying phenomena," wrote Elder Talmage, "There was a violent earthquake; the rocks of the mighty hills were disrupted, and many graves were torn open... the veil of the temple which hung between the Holy Place and the Holy of Holies was rent [torn] from top to bottom, and the interior, which none but the high priest had been permitted to see, was thrown open to common gaze. It was the rending [yielding] of Judaism, the consummation of the Mosaic dispensation, and the inauguration of Christianity under apostolic administration." [103]

We can only imagine the range of emotions experienced, and the sorrowful tears shed, by all these faithful women—especially by His beloved mother and Mary Magdalene, following the physical death of Jesus, and the terror each experienced by this earthquake—which none of the Gospel writers have recorded how long it lasted or the damage it caused—and the veil of the temple being torn from top to bottom. When the earth finally stopped shaking, and with awareness that Jesus was dead, the urgent need for these faithful women was to immediately take care of His body before the Sabbath day commenced.

As to what transpired next, Farrar wrote this description: "The sun was now on the edge of the horizon, and the Sabbath day was near [at sunset it would start]...The Jews had taken every precaution to prevent the ceremonial pollution of a day so sacred and were anxious that immediately after the death of a victim had been secured, their bodies should be taken from the cross...The dead body of Jesus was left hanging till the last, because a person who could not easily be slighted [offended] had gone to obtain leave from Pilate to dispose of it as he wished. This was Joseph of Arimathea, a rich man, of high character and blameless life, and a distinguished member of the Sanhedrin...Pilate had no difficulty in sanctioning... the burial of the dead. He was, however, amazed at the speediness with which the death [of Jesus] had [transpired], and sending for the centurion [the man in charge for the crucifixion of Jesus], asked whether it had taken place sufficiently long [since] to distinguish it from a faint or swoon [blackout]. On ascertaining that such was the fact [that Jesus was dead], he once assigned the body, doubtless with some real satisfaction, to the care of this [Joseph]" [See Matthew 27:57-61; Mark 15:42-47; Luke 23:50-56]. [104]

To help one understand more fully what transpired next, Alfred Edersheim [who Elder Bruce R. McConkie periodically quoted in his *The Mortal Messiah* series] wrote this informative description:

"The Cross was lowered and laid on the ground; the cruel nails drawn out, and the ropes unloosed. Joseph, with those who attended him, 'wrapped' the Sacred Body 'in a clean linen cloth,' and rapidly carried It [the body of Jesus] to the rock-hewn tomb in the garden close by. Such a rock-hewn tomb or cave...had niches...where the dead were laid...None of Christ's former disciples seem to have taken part in the burying. [Only one is mentioned:] John [who] may have with-drawn to bring tidings to, and to comfort the Vir-gin-Mother; the others also, [other women] that had 'stood afar off, beholding,' appear to have left.

"Only a few faithful ones, notably among them Mary Magdalene and the other Mary, the mother of Joses, stood over against the tomb, watching at some distance where and how the body of Jesus was laid...From where they stood they could only have had a dim view of what passed within the court, and this may explain how, on their return, they 'prepared spices and ointments'...they hoped to [administer to] the Dead [Jesus] after the Sab-bath was past." [105]

Providing additional information, Elder James E. Talmage expressed this view: "The body was removed from the cross; and in preparing it for the tomb, Joseph was assisted by Nicodemus, another member of the Sanhedrin, the same who had come to Jesus by night three years before... Nicodemus brought a large quantity of myrrh and aloes, about a hundredweight...These two revering disciples wrapped the Lord's body in clean linen, 'with the spices, as the manner of the Jews is to bury;' and then laid it in a new sepul-cher, hewn in the rock. The tomb was in a garden, not far from Calvary, and was the property of Joseph. Because of the nearness of the Sabbath the interment had to be made with haste; the door of the sepulcher was closed; a large stone was rolled against it; and thus laid away the body was left to rest. Some of the devoted women, particularly Mary Magdalene, and 'the other Mary,' who was the mother of James and Joses, had watched the entombment from a distance; and when it was completed 'they returned, and prepared spices and ointments; and rested the sabbath day according to the commandment'" [106] [Matthew 27:57-61; Mark 15:42-47; Luke 23:50-56; John 19:38-42].

<u>AT THE TOMB</u>

On Saturday evening, the Jewish Sabbath had passed, and the Roman guard kept watch over the sealed sepulcher, for fear that the body of Jesus might be taken by His faithful disciples, who would "say unto the people, He is risen from the dead." While it was still dark outside, but starting to dawn, the earth began to shake, and an angel of the Lord descended in glory, who rolled back the massive stone covering the entrance of the tomb and then sat upon it. His countenance was like lightning, and his clothing was as white as snow. The soldiers were paralyzed with fear and fell to the earth as dead men. When they recovered from their fright, they fled in terror (See Matthew 27:56-66; 28:2-4).

From Mark's record, it is written that when the Sabbath was past [which was Saturday for the Jews] "Mary Magdalene, and Mary the mother of James, [who possibly is the mother of Jesus—see John 19:25] and Salome [who is the sister of Mary, the mother of Jesus—see also John 19:25], had bought sweet spices, that they might come and anoint him [Jesus]." [Mark 16:1. Italics added].

On the way, these women sorrowfully conversed and realized the difficulty of entering the tomb. "And they said among themselves, 'Who shall roll us away from the stone from the door of the sepulcher?'"

When they neared the tomb, they saw that the large stone had been rolled away. Upon entering the tomb, they saw a young man [according to the Joseph Smith Translation, it was two angels] and "the angels said unto them, Be not affrighted; ye seek Jesus of Nazareth, who was crucified; he is risen; he is not here; behold the place where they laid him; And go your way, tell his disciples and Peter, that he goeth before you into Galilee; there shall ye see him as he said unto you. And they went out quickly, and fled...for they trembled and were amazed..." (See Mark 16: 3-8; Joseph Smith Translation Mark 16: 3-6).

CHRIST APPEARED TO MARY

"It is now Sunday, April 9, A.D. 30—the 17th of Nisan—the day of the resurrection," wrote Elder Bruce R. McConkie. "It is the first day of the week— 'according to the Jewish reckoning the third day from His Death.' According to Jewish tradition, 'the soul hovered round the body till the third day, when it finally parted from its earthly tabernacle,' and it was on that day that 'corruption was supposed to begin.' Up to that time relatives and friends were in the habit of 'going to the grave...so as to make sure those laid there were really dead' (Edersheim 2:630-31)." [107]

After Peter and John ran to the tomb and entered the sepulcher, they saw the folded linen clothes and the napkin that had been placed on the head of Jesus. John speaking for himself, and his fellow apostles, wrote: "For as yet they knew not the scripture, that he must rise again from the dead." Then, not fully knowing what to do, these "disciples went away unto their own home. (John 20:3-10)."

It is apparent that the sorrowful Magdalene had followed the two apostles back to the tomb. While Peter and John were within the sepulcher, Mary had stayed outside, weeping. After these men left—we appropriately wonder if these three spoke to one another—"she stooped down [bent down], and looked into the sepulcher," and to her surprise, she saw "two angels in white sitting," and one was "at the head, and the other at the feet, where the body of Jesus had lain." It appears that in unison these heavenly messengers asked in tenderness, "Woman, why weepest thou?" No thought of the Lord's restoration to life appears to have found place in her grief-stricken body and mind; she only knew that the body of her Messiah—her beloved Friend and Great Healer—had been taken or moved from the tomb. In reply to these angels, she sincerely expressed these heart-felt and sorrowful words, "Because they have taken away my Lord, and I know not where they have laid him." Turning from the tomb, which was still illuminated from these angelic person-ages, she "saw Jesus standing, and knew not that it was Jesus." He tenderly asked, "Woman, why weepest thou? Whom seekest thou?" (John 20:11-15).

"Scarcely lifting her tearful countenance to look at the Questioner," wrote Elder Talmage, "but vaguely supposing that He was the caretaker of the garden, and that He might have knowledge of what had been done with the body of her Lord, she exclaimed, 'Sir, if thou have borne him hence, tell me where thou hast laid him,' she pleaded. It was Jesus to whom she [spoke], her beloved Lord, though she knew it not." [By a divine law,

Jesus was able to disguise His identity from this faithful follower] One word from His living lips changed her agonized grief into ecstatic joy. 'Jesus said unto her, *Mary*.' The voice, the tone, the tender accent she had heard and loved in the earlier days lifted her from the despairing depths into which she had sunk. She turned, and saw the Lord [Again by a divine law, Jesus allowed His beloved follower to see His Resurrected Body]. In a transport [with soul-filled exuberance], she reached out her arms to embrace Him, uttering only the endearing and worshipful word, 'Rabboni,' meaning 'My beloved Master' (John 20: 14-16)." [108]

As it pertains to "divine law," the following revelations were given to the Prophet Joseph Smith: (1) "Wherefore, verily I say unto you that all things unto me are spiritual, *and not at any time have I given unto you law which was temporal*; neither any man, nor the children of men; neither Adam... whom I created" (Doctrine and Covenants 29:34. Italics added). In addition: (2) "And again, verily I say unto you, *he hath given a law unto all things*, by which they move in their times and their seasons" (Doctrine and Covenants 88:42. Italics added).

As to Jesus disguising His identity, the following examples will support this view: (1) While two men were walking to "the village called Emmaus," the Resurrected Lord "*appeared in another form unto two of them* (Mark 16:12-13. Italics added); (2) And while these two men "communed together and reasoned, Jesus himself drew near, and went with them. *But their eyes were holden that they should not know him...*" Later, "as he [Jesus] sat at meat with them, he took bread, and blessed it, and brake, and gave to them. *And their eyes were opened, and they knew him; and he vanished out of their sight*" (John 24:13-16, 30-31. Italics added).

Returning to our narrative, the Lord gently answered Mary: "Hold me not; for I am not yet ascended to my Father; but go to my brethren [His Apostles], and say unto them, I ascend unto my [literal] Father, and your [Heavenly] Father; and to my God, and your God" (John 11:17).

"We cannot believe that the caution which withheld from Jesus the embrace of Mary," wrote Elder McConkie, "was anything more than the building of a proper wall of reserve between intimates who are now on two sides of the veil...But perhaps there was more in Jesus' statement than Mary related or than John recorded, for in a short time we shall see a group of faithful women hold Jesus by his feet as they worship him...The King James Version quotes Jesus as saying, 'Touch me not.' The Joseph Smith Translation reads: 'Hold me not.' [20:17] Various translations from the Greek render the passage as 'Do not cling to me' or 'Do not hold me.' Some give the meaning as

'Do not cling to me any longer,' or 'Do not hold me any longer.' Some speak of ceasing to hold him or cling to him, leaving the inference that Mary was already holding him. There is valid reason for supposing that the thought conveyed to Mary by the Risen Lord was to this effect: 'You cannot hold me here, for I am going to ascend to my Father.' But the great message that was preserved for us is Jesus' eternal relationship to his Father. 'My' Father and 'your' Father—Elohim is the Father of all men in the spirit, and of the Lord Jesus is an added and special sense. He is the Father of both Jesus's spirit and his body. 'My' God and 'your' God—and again Elohim is the God of all men, but in Jesus's case, though he himself is a God and has all power, though he is a member of the very Godhead itself, yet is he everlastingly in subjection to the same God who is our Father.

"After these things Mary Magdalene, as he had directed, went to the Twelve [Apostles], told them all that happened, and bore them this testimony: 'I have seen the Lord!' [John 20:18].

"For reasons of his own, the Risen Lord singled out Mary Magdalene to be the first witness, in point of time, of his resurrection. She was the first mortal of all mortals ever to see a resurrected person...

"Then, still in his own infinite wisdom, Jesus

chose to appear to and be handled by a group of other women—all before he came even to Peter and the rest of the Twelve, all before his appearances to the hundreds of brethren who were privileged to see him before that day on the Mount of Olives when he ascended to reign on the right hand of the Everlasting Power forever.

"These other women included Mary the mother of Joses; Joanna, evidently the wife of Chuza, Herod's steward (Luke 8:3); and Salome, the mother of James and John. Among them were women who had been with Jesus in Galilee. Certainly, the beloved sisters from Bethany were there; and, in general, the group would have been made up of the same ones who had [gathered] in sorrow around the cross. Their total number may well have been in the dozens or scores" [109] [See Matthew 28:1, 5-10; Mark 16:1-8; Luke 24:1-10].

ADDITIONAL EVENTS TRANSPIRED

Matthew records that the ancient Saints were resurrected with Jesus: "And the graves were opened; and many bodies of the saints which slept arose, and came out of the graves after his resurrection, and went into the holy city, and appeared unto many" (27:52-53; Joseph Smith Translation 27:56). This is all that is written of this significant event. As to what transpired with these resurrected Saints, nothing has been revealed.

As was previously written in the section about Translated Beings, it is important to note that one of the teachings of the gospel of Jesus Christ is that all the righteous Saints from the time of Adam and Eve up to the time of the Lord's resurrection came forth with Christ at his resurrection from the dead (See Doctrine and Covenants 133:54-55. Italics added). If we might indulge in speculation, this author supposes that these people were taken into Paradise to await the day when every individual will be assigned a kingdom of glory, based on her or his individual righteousness (See Doctrine and Covenants 76; 88;101;105;131;132;137).

As Jesus Christ was the first person on this earth to be resurrected from the dead, it is important to learn of teachings surrounding this glorious event. In LDS beliefs it is written: "'For as in Adam all die,' the apostle Paul declared, 'even so in Christ shall all be made alive' (1 Corinthians 15:22). Because Jesus Christ, the Only Begotten Son of God, forever broke the bands of death and as the risen Lord became 'the firstfruits of them that slept' (1 Corinthians 15:20), all mankind will be literally resurrected from death to immortality, from corruptibility to incorruptibility (1 Corinthians 15:54). The Prophet Joseph Smith taught that the resurrection of the dead is very basic to our beliefs and that it should be taught 'among the first principles of the Gospel of Jesus Christ.'" [110]

GAINING A SPIRITUAL TESTIMONY

The following statements are from Elder McConkie, who explained that for "some years I have sought to learn all that a mortal can of the life of Jesus Christ—the greatest life ever lived—of his words and works in the days of his life on earth, *the atonement he wrought*, and the *glory that was his in life, and in death, and in living again*." [111]

Please know that this author has taken the liberty of selecting various parts of his wonderful writing:

"We have a glorious message to take to the world. It's a message of salvation, a message of joy and hope and glad tidings. It is spiritual. And immediately the question arises as to how you establish the truth and divinity of a spiritual message. How do you prove spiritual truths? *How do you prove the resurrection of Jesus Christ?...*

"*I believe that a testimony of Jesus Christ depends on a belief in the resurrection.* If Jesus rose from the dead, he is the Son of God! If he is the Son of God, his gospel is true. If his gospel is true, men [mankind] must believe and obey or their possible exaltation is in peril!...*And how* do *you prove the resurrection!* As we are going to [read], *you prove it by testimony.*

"Paul testified that Jesus Christ was 'declared to be the Son of God with power, according to the spirit of holiness, *by the resurrection from the dead'* (See Rom. 1:1-4)... 'And that he was buried, and that he rose again the third day according to the scriptures'...

"Sometime early Sunday morning, Jesus rose from the dead. We do not know the time, but the record says that 'when it was yet dark' (John 20:11), Mary Magdalene came to the tomb...[looking in] she found not the body of the Lord Jesus. She was told by the angels to tell Peter that Christ was risen...Either she went back and told Peter and came again, or she went out of the tomb then and saw the risen Lord. In any event, she was the first mortal to see a resurrected person...' [This was **His first appearance**]...

"'As it began to dawn' (Matt. 28:1), other women arrived, apparently in a group... they met Jesus and they threw their arms around his feet. *Now that has to mean that they felt the nail marks in his hands and perhaps more.* We do not know what transpired there, other than that Jesus directed again the same message the angels had given the woman from Magdala [which is Mary Magdalene]. Jesus said, 'Tell Peter and the brethren that I am going before them into Galilee' (see Matt. 28:10. ***Now that's two appearances of the risen Lord on Easter morning.'***

"The next appearance, although we cannot document this with accuracy...was to Peter and we suppose it was because Peter was to be the president of the Church; he held the keys of the kingdom... [See Luke 24:33-35; and from what Paul wrote—1 Cor. 15:5].

"The next appearance, the details of which we know, occurred in Emmaus (see Luke 24:13)... One of them was named Cleopas; we assume the other one was Luke, since he alone recorded what took place...It may be that this conversation lasted as long as two hours... Then he vanished [See Mark 16:12-13; Luke 24:13-32; Joseph Smith Translation 24:15, 30]...

"That's four appearances. Those two disciples returned immediately from Emmaus to Jerusalem. They went to a place that is called the upper room...there was a large congregation present. The only ones we usually talk about are the ten Apostles, but there were others, and this leads us to presume that among the others there may have been women...When they entered the room, someone was bearing testimony that the Lord had appeared to Simon, showing...that appearance had preceded this hour at least.

"As they were going forward with their meal and with their testimonies, the account says Jesus himself stood in the midst of them. Then it says 'they were terrified and affrighted, and supposed that they had seen a spirit' (Luke 24:37), which is a natural conclusion because they were in a barred room, the door was closed, and here someone had materialized who had come either through the ceiling or the wall. And he said unto them: 'Why are ye troubled and why do thoughts arise in your hearts?'

"Behold my hands and my feet, that it is I myself: handle me, and see; for a spirit hath not flesh and bones, as ye see me have' (Luke 24:38-39).

"And without any question, they then felt the nail marks in his hands and feet, and they thrust their hands into the spear wound in his side...[and he ate] 'a piece of a broiled fish, and of an honeycomb' (Luke 24:42-43) And some other conversations ensued.

"Ten of the Twelve were there. For what reasons we do not know, Thomas was absent...

"One week later, again on the Sabbath... apparently in the upper room, the same...group assembled. Jesus appeared, and he said to Thomas, 'Stretch forth thine hand, and feel the prints of the nails in my hands and in my feet, and be not faithless, but believing' (see John 20:27)...And we suppose that he accepted the invitation and felt and handled as the others had felt and handled the previous week...

"The next appearance chronologically of which we have record was on the shore of the lake of Tiberias (the Sea of Galilee)...Only seven of the Twelve are present, five of whom are named...(see John 21:5-6; Matt. 4:21).

"...The next appearance was on that mountain in Galilee...more than five hundred brethren were there. This leads us to assume that there must have been women present also...that's the occasion when he issued the decree the Twelve should go into all the world and preach the gospel to every creature (see Mark 16:15). And many other things, without question, were said.

"**Now that's eight appearances**. After that he appeared to James [who is his half-brother, and an Apostle] (see 1 Cor. 15:7). [Making it the ninth appearance.]

"**The tenth appearance** of which the New Testament speaks is the ascension... *forty days after his resurrection he appeared to the Eleven* [Apostles]. They apparently walked out to the Mount of Olives; and while they were on the Mount of Olives, they had the conversation about the restoration of the kingdom of Israel. And then he ascended...(Acts 1:11)."

"...The way Peter and the ancients proved that Jesus was the Son of God, and therefore that the gospel which he taught was the plan of salvation, *was to establish that he rose from the dead*. And the way you prove that a man rises from the dead, because it's a spiritual thing is to *bear witness by the power of the Spirit of knowledge that* is *personal and real and literal to you...*

"The message of salvation is proclaimed by witnesses, and this segment of the life of the Lord Jesus sets a pattern and shows what we have to do when we carry the message of the Restoration to our Father's other children." [112]

Clothing

Now that we have explored Jesus's agonizing death and triumphal resurrection, we will examine what our journey is with regard to clothing for both spirits and resurrected beings.

Elder Wilford Woodruff wrote of his visit with President John Taylor to the quarterly conference in Logan, Utah, sometime later in the month of April 1882:

President Taylor revealed that "when we go to the spirit world, *we go naked*, as we came into the world, or if we get any clothing it is as much by our dependence upon others as when we were born into this world. If we get a mansion in our Father's Kingdom, we shall also be dependent upon Him for it." [113]

This teaching from President Taylor makes

perfect sense for this author, for we take nothing from this earth when we die a natural or temporal death. It is noted that there are many men and women who earnestly strive to dress modestly throughout her or his mortal life. These individuals can be assured that when they enter the world of spirits that he or she will immediately be given a robe to protect decency and modesty.

The clothing that both spirits and resurrected personages wear is described in different ways. In a dream-vision, Daniel was able to see Adam, the first man on this earth, described as the "*Ancient of days* did sit, *whose garment was white as snow*" (Daniel 7:9. Italics added).

John the Revelator described the dress of the righteous martyrs slain for the testimony of our Lord, saying that, "*white robes were given unto every one of them*" (Revelation 6:9-11. Italics added).

In Lehi's vision of the tree of life, he says "I saw a man, and he was *dressed in a white robe*; and he came and stood before me. And it came to pass that he spake unto me, and bade me follow him" (1 Nephi 8:5-6. Italics added).

After Jesus had been crucified and his body had been laid in a borrowed tomb, it is written that "Mary [Magdalene] stood without at the sepulcher weeping: and as she wept, she stooped down, and looked into the sepulcher, And seeth *two angels in white* sitting, the one at the head, and the other at the feet, where the body of Jesus had lain" (John 20:11-12. Italics added). Not only were these angels illuminated with white light, but they also wore white robes.

The Prophet Joseph Smith gave a detailed description of the clothing worn by the Angel Moroni: "He *had on a loose robe of most exquisite whiteness*. It was a whiteness beyond anything earthly I had ever seen; nor do I believe that any earthly thing could be made to appear so exceedingly white and brilliant... I could discover that *he had no other clothing on but this robe*, as it was open, so that I could see into his bosom" (Joseph Smith—History 1:31. Italics added).

On March 15, 1848, Elder Wilford Woodruff, then a member of the Quorum of the Twelve Apostles, described the following scenes he saw in a "remarkable dream in which he passed in spirit through the air from state to state [meaning being bodily transported], escaped from his enemies and passed on to heaven."

"I saw," he says, "Joseph and Hyrum [Smith] and many others of the Latter-day Saints who had died. The innumerable company of souls which I saw seemed to be preparing for some grand and important event which I could not understand. Many were engaged in making crowns of the Saints. *They were all dressed in white robes, both male and female.*" [114]

Priesthood Keys

With this explanation about clothing, we now turn our attention to an important question that was asked: "Priesthood keys: What are they and why do they matter?" From a study by Mark A. Mathews, he provides these well-written answers:

"'Priesthood keys' is a term that many have heard used in Church discussion but is not always well defined or understood. If we do not understand what priesthood keys are then we can't fully appreciate why they matter and why we should follow those who hold them.

"As a BYU instructor, I often begin a discussion on priesthood keys by asking two related questions: What is the priesthood? And what are priesthood keys? Most students can confidently define priesthood as 'the authority and power that God gives to man to act in all things for the salvation of man.' And recognize that 'male members of the Church…hold the priesthood' (Priesthood, Guide to the Scriptures).

"However, when faced with the second question, very few feel comfortable explaining what keys are. *In my experience, the simplest way to understand what priesthood keys are is to discover who holds them. Priesthood keys are held by priesthood presidents. Once this is clear, it is obvious that priesthood keys are the right to preside, direct, and control the priesthood within a leader's jurisdiction.* The scriptures define priesthood keys simply as 'the right of presidency' (see D&C 107:8; D&C 68:17).

"As explained in Guide to the Scriptures, 'Keys are the *rights of presidency,* or the power given to man by God to direct, control, and govern God's priesthood on earth. Priesthood holders called to positions of presidency [i.e. Priesthood presidents] receive keys from those in authority over them. Priesthood holders use the priesthood only within the limits outlined by those who hold the keys' (Keys of the Priesthood, Guide to the Scriptures, emphasis added).

Giving further examples, he explains:

"The President of the Church delegates priesthood keys to other priesthood leaders so they can preside in their areas of responsibility. Priesthood keys are bestowed on presidents of temples, missions, stakes, and districts; bishops; branch presidents; and quorum presidents. This presiding authority is valid only for the designated responsibilities and within the geographic jurisdiction of each leader's calling. When priesthood leaders are released from their callings, they no longer hold the associated keys.

He next explains who does not receive priesthood keys:

"Counselors to priesthood leaders do not receive keys. They are set apart and function in their callings by assignment and delegated authority.

"All ward and stake auxiliary organizations operate under the direction of the bishop or stake president, who holds the keys to preside. Auxiliary presidents and their counselors do not receive keys. They receive delegated authority to function in their callings. (Handbook 2 2.1.1)

Brother Mathews then makes this interesting observation about women:

"Interestingly, if women set apart to serve in auxiliary presidencies have 'delegated authority,' it means they have priesthood authority in their calling. As President Dallin H. Oaks explained, 'We are not accustomed to speaking of women having the authority of the priesthood in their Church callings, but what other authority can it be? When a woman—young or old—is set apart... she is given priesthood authority to perform a priesthood function' (President Dallin H. Oaks, *Ensign* May 2014).

<u>KEYS OF THE KINGDOM</u>

These keys are often called the "keys of the kingdom" because "'the kingdom of God on earth is The Church of Jesus Christ of Latter-day Saints" (Kingdom of God, Guide to the Scriptures). Handbook 2 explains clearly who holds these keys and how they operate:

"Jesus Christ holds all the keys of the priesthood pertaining to His Church. He has conferred upon each of His Apostles all the keys that pertain to the kingdom of God on earth. The senior living Apostle, the President of the Church, is the only person on earth authorized to exercise all priesthood keys.

"Seventies act by assignment and by the delegation of authority from the First Presidency and Quorum of the Twelve Apostles. Area Presidents are assigned to administer areas under the authorization of the First Presidency and the Twelve. The Presidency of the Seventy are set apart and are given the keys to preside over the Quorums of Seventy. (Handbook 2 2.1.1)

"Because this is Jesus Christ's Church, He

always holds the 'keys of the kingdom' to preside as the head of the Church. These keys of universal presiding authority are also conferred on each of His Apostles when they join the Quorum of the Twelve. By conferring these keys upon each of the Apostles, it safeguards the keys so they are never lost from the earth at the unexpected death of the president of the Church [therefore,] each Apostle can act as a prophet, seer, and revelator to the Church, exercising their keys to receive revelation and teach with authority in their Apostolic service.

"However, although each Apostle holds all priesthood keys, there are 'limits or constraints' on how they can use them. They must exercise their keys only 'in harmony with the other [Apostles] and under the direction of the President of the Church' (Elder Dale G. Renlund, The Melchizedek Priesthood p. 29). Because priesthood keys are the right of presidency, they can only be fully exercised by one person at a time, namely the President of the Church who is the senior Apostle. He alone is the only one who holds *and is authorized to exercise* all priesthood keys. As the Lord has explained, there is never but one on the earth at a time on whom this power and the keys of this priesthood are conferred' (D&C 132:7)..."[115]

With these well-explained points, and knowing that Jesus Christ was the first person on this earth to be resurrected from the dead, it is important to learn of teachings surrounding this glorious event. In LDS beliefs it is written: "'For as in Adam all die,' the apostle Paul declared, 'even so in Christ shall all be made alive' (1 Corinthians 15:22). Because Jesus Christ, the Only Begotten Son of God, forever broke the bands of death and as the risen Lord became 'the firstfruits of them that slept' (1 Corinthians 15:20), all mankind will be literally resurrected from death to immortality, from corruptibility to incorruptibility (1 Corinthians 15:54). Again, the Prophet Joseph Smith taught that the resurrection of the dead is so foundational to our beliefs that it should be taught 'among the first principles of the Gospel of Jesus Christ.'" [116]

<u>KIRTLAND TEMPLE</u>

With this understanding, we now turn our attention to *four glorious visions which transpired in the Kirtland Temple on Easter Sunday, April 3, 1836.* This series of visions transpired a week after the Temple was dedicated on March 27, 1836 (Doctrine and Covenants 109, Heading). By way of introduction, the Prophet Joseph Smith stated: "Sunday, 3—Attended meeting in the Lord's house, and assisted the other Presidents of the Church in seating the congregation, and then became an attentive listener to the preaching from the stand. . . [also] to an attentive audience of about one thousand persons...After [the congregation received] the Lord's supper [emblems of the sacrament], I retired to the pulpit, the veils [canvas curtains that were used to divide the large meeting room into classrooms] being dropped [down], and bowed myself, with Oliver Cowdery, in solemn and silent prayer. After rising from prayer, the following vision was opened to both of us (*History of the Church*, 2: 434-435; See also Doctrine and Covenants 110).

<u>VISION OF THE SAVIOR</u>

"The veil was taken from our minds, and the eyes of our understanding were opened.

"*We saw the Lord* [Jesus Christ] standing upon the breastwork of the pulpit [a small wall that extends from both sides of the pulpit], before us; and under his feet was a paved work of pure gold, in color like amber [symbolic of divine glory—See Ezekial 1:3-4].

"His eyes were as a flame of fire [not literally, but symbolic of celestial glory—See Hebrew 12:29, Deuteronomy 4:24]; the hair of his head was white like the pure snow [probably literally, and symbolic of the Savior's power to cleanse individuals from sin—compare Isaiah 1:18; Revelation 7:14];

his countenance shone above the brightness of the sun [See Doctrine and Covenants 5:19, 65:5]; and his voice was as the sound of the rushing of great waters, even the voice of Jehovah [not literally, but symbolic of the majesty of his voice], saying:

"I am the first and the last [Under the direction of God the Father, He is our Savior and Redeemer]; I am he who liveth [He is resurrected, and came forth from the tomb], I am he who was slain [He was crucified on the cruel cross]; I am your advocate with the Father [meaning that He pleads the cause of the righteous in the courts above—See Doctrine and Covenants 29:5; 32:3, 45:3; Moroni 7:28].

Next, His power to bless and purify Joseph and Oliver: "Behold, your sins are forgiven you; you are clean before me; therefore, lift up your heads and rejoice. [We can imagine—but not fully know—how these words brought great comfort and solace to these humble men].

With kindness, the Lord said, "Let the hearts of your brethren rejoice, and let the hearts of all my people rejoice, who have, with their might, built this house [Kirtland Temple] to my name."

As to the plea that the Prophet previously asked in his dedicatory prayer, a week previous, the Lord stated: "For behold, I have accepted this house, and my name shall be here; and I will manifest myself to my people in mercy in this house.

Speaking of those who worthily enter the Temple, the Lord said that He will appear and speak unto them with His own voice. Next, the Savior gave a prophecy about the Kirtland Temple: "And the fame of this house shall spread to foreign lands; and this is the beginning of the blessings which shall be poured out upon the heads of my people. Even So. Amen." (Doctrine and Covenants 110:1-10. Italics added). Then, this glorious appearance ended.

<u>VISION OF MOSES</u>

"After this vision closed, the heavens were again opened unto us; *and Moses appeared before us*, and committed unto us, the keys of the gathering of Israel from the four parts of the earth, and the leading of the ten tribes from the land of the north." (Doctrine and Covenants 110:11).

During his presidency as the seventeenth President of The Church of Jesus Christ of Latter-day Saints, President Russell M. Nelson often spoke and wrote about the gathering of Israel. To briefly state some of his teachings, he wrote: "For centuries, prophets have foreseen and foretold the gathering that is happening right now! As an essential prelude to the Second Coming of the Lord Jesus Christ, this gathering is *the most* important work in the world. As members of The Church of Jesus Christ of Latter-day Saints, or 'latter-day covenant Israel,' we have been charged to assist the Lord with this pivotal work."

Providing additional insight, he wrote: "When we speak of gathering Israel on both sides of the veil, we are referring, of course, to missionary, temple, and family history work. We are also referring to building faith and testimony in the hearts of those with whom we live, work, and serve...*Anytime* we do *anything* that helps *anyone*—on either side of the veil—to make and keep their covenants with God, we are helping to gather Israel. It is as simple and profound as that." [117]

After Moses delivered his keys, he was no longer seen by the Prophet Joseph Smith or Oliver Cowdery.

VISION OF ELIAS

It is important for the reader to know the following: "There are several uses of this word in scriptures [Elias]. It is the New Testament (Greek) form of Elijah (Hebrew), as in Luke 4:25-26; James 5:17, and Matt.17: 1-4. Elias in these instances can only be the ancient prophet Elijah whose ministry is recorded in 1 and 2 Kings.

"Elias is also a title for one who is a forerunner;

for example, John the Baptist, as in JST Matt. 11: 13-15; JST Matt. 17: 10-14, and JST John 1:20-28... One as a *preparer* and the other a *restorer*. [Notice this distinction:] John was sent to prepare the way for Jesus. [Then] Jesus Himself being the Restorer who brought back the gospel and the Melchizedek Priesthood...(JST John 1:20-28).

"The title Elias has also been applied to many others for specific missions or restorative functions. For example, John the Revelator (D&C 77:14) and Noah or Gabriel (Luke 1:11-20; D&C 110:12).

[Note these words:] "A man called Elias apparently lived in mortality in the days of Abraham, who committed the dispensation of the gospel of Abraham to Joseph Smith and Oliver Cowdery in the Kirtland (Ohio) Temple on April 3, 1836 (D&C 110:12). We have no specific information as to the details of his mortal life or ministry." [118] It has further been written: "*A prophet called Esaias or Elias who apparently lived in the days of Abraham*" (D&C 84:11-13; 110:12). [119]

From this, it appears evident that the prophet who appeared in the Kirtland Temple was either called "Esaias" or "Elias." Speaking to the Prophet and Oliver, this man said, "that in us and our seed all generations after us should be blessed" (Doctrine and Covenants 110:12).

By way of clarification, Brother David J. Ridges

has explained that the "'blessings of Abraham, Isaac, and Jacob' (as often mentioned in patriarchal blessings) definitely have reference to exaltation, since all three of these ancient prophets have already become gods (see D&C 132:37)." [120]

As written in LDS beliefs, "The Abrahamic Covenant is an important aspect of the new and everlasting covenant, the fullness of the gospel of Jesus Christ. God entered into a covenant with Abraham, promising him and his posterity would receive the gospel (Galatians 3:8), the priesthood, eternal life, and a land of inheritance (Genesis 13:14-16; 15:1-6; 17:1-7; JST, Genesis 13; 15; Abraham 2:8-11, 19). These promises are often called 'the promises made to the fathers' (D&C 2:2; see also 27:10; 98:32), inasmuch as they were perpetuated through Isaac, Jacob, Joseph, and their descendants." [121]

After receiving his keys, Elias was no longer visible.

VISION OF ELIJAH

The record states: "After this vision had closed, another great and glorious vision burst upon us; for Elijah the prophet, who was taken to heaven without tasting death, stood before us, and said:

"Behold the time has fully come, which was spoken by the mouth of Malachi [See

4:5-6]—testifying that he [Elijah] should be sent, before the great and dreadful day of the Lord come [the Second Coming]—To turn the hearts of the fathers to the children, and the children to the fathers, lest the whole earth be smitten with a curse—Therefore, the keys of this dispensation are committed into your hands; and by this ye may know that the great and dreadful day of the Lord is near, even at the doors." (Doctrine and Covenants 110: 13-16).

The Prophet Joseph Smith explained the significance of Elijah's mission in this final dispensation of the fulness of times: "The spirit, power, and calling of Elijah is, that ye have power to hold the key of the revelation, ordinances, oracles, powers and endowment of the fulness of the Melchizedek Priesthood and of the Kingdom of God on the earth; and to receive, obtain, and perform all the ordinances belonging to the kingdom of God, even unto the turning of the hearts of the fathers unto the children, and the hearts of the children unto the fathers, even those who are in heaven...

"...This, the spirit of Elijah, that we redeem our dead, and connect ourselves with our fathers which are in heaven, and seal up our dead to come forth in the first resurrection; and here we want the power of Elijah to seal those who dwell on earth to those who dwell in heaven. This is the power of Elijah and the keys of the kingdom of Jehovah." [122]

Providing additional information, Elder McConkie explained the ministry of Elias and Elijah:

"Thus, through the joint ministry of Elijah, who brought the sealing power, and Elias, *who restored the marriage discipline of Abraham*, the way was prepared for the planting in the hearts of the children of the promises made to the fathers (D&C 2:2)." [123]

At a meeting for Temple workers, Elder McConkie spoke these clarifying words: "The Lord sent Elias, and he sent Elijah. And when Elias came, he brought the gospel of Abraham, not the gospel of Christ, the gospel of Abraham, the divine commission that God gave Abraham, the marriage discipline that God gave Abraham. [Note these profound words:] *Elias restored celestial marriage*, and *Elijah came and brought the sealing power so the ordinance [of celestial marriage] would be binding on earth and sealed in heaven*, and it takes the ministry of both of them to accomplish the purposes of the Lord." [124]

After this vision, the Prophet Joseph Smith and Oliver Cowdery were left to ponder and discuss the greatness of these four heavenly visits. As to what transpired with Moses, Elias, and Elijah, it has not been revealed.

Keys Of The Resurrection

DUE TO IMPORTANT PRIESTHOOD KEYS HAVING been bestowed in the Kirtland Temple, we now turn our attention to a seldom discussed—but deeply fascinating—doctrine unique to the theology of The Church of Jesus Christ of Latter-day Saints. This teaching may be unfamiliar to many members of the Church, yet it is firmly grounded in scripture and teachings from prophets and apostles. Drawing on inspired sources from this final dispensation, let us begin our study of *keys of the resurrection.*

NATHAN'S PATRIARCHAL BLESSING

When my youngest son, Nathan, was seventeen years of age, he desired and received a patriarchal blessing on May 20, 2001, from a righteous patriarch, Vincent E. Erickson. In one part of Nathan's blessing the following was spoken and later written: "Because of your righteous efforts and the successful accomplishment of your life's mission upon this earth, you will be blessed to come forth in the morning of the resurrection. [Note these words:] Jesus Christ will personally meet you and embrace you. He will thank you for your service to Him and will bestow upon you *the keys of resurrection*, that you might bring your eternal helpmeet from the grave." What a tremendous promise, based upon Nathan's faithfulness!

This was the first time that this author paid attention to this doctrine, *keys of the resurrection*. It was not until October 2025 that I diligently studied this intriguing teaching. Together, let us learn what has been spoken or written by the Lord's chosen servants.

EARLY LEADERS OF THE CHURCH

With reference to the teachings of the early leaders of The Church of Jesus Christ of Latter-day Saints, who were called during the administration of the Prophet Joseph Smith, Elder Bruce R. McConkie wrote this very informative view: *"Joseph Smith and the early brethren in this dispensation knew much that we do not know and will not know until we attain the same spiritual stature that was theirs."* [125]

With this declaration written, we begin with two teachings spoken by President Brigham Young, second president of the Church.

In a discourse that was given in the Tabernacle on March 25, 1860, he began by saying: "I will make a few remarks upon the portion of Scripture quoted by Brother [Orson] Hyde:

"Jesus said unto her [Martha], I am the resurrection, and the life: he that believeth in me, though he were dead, yet shall he live: And whosoever liveth and believeth in me shall never die." [See John 11:25. This statement is regarding the death of her brother, Lazarus.]

President Young explained: "In the Scripture above quoted, the death spoken of is a death that the intelligent being undergoes...The death that Jesus referred to had no reference to these bodies going into the grave. He is the life and the light. He is the resurrection; he is the power; and 'if you believe in me,' says Jesus, 'you shall live forever—you shall be prepared to dwell with me in my Father's kingdom.'

Later in his discourse, President Young revealed this doctrine: "After the spirit leaves the body, it remains without a tabernacle [physical body] in the spirit world until the Lord, by his law that he has ordained, brings to pass the resurrection of the dead. *When the angel who holds the keys of the resurrection shall sound his trumpet*, then the peculiar fundamental particles that organized our bodies here [on earth], if we do honor to them, though they be deposited in the depths of the sea, and though one particle is in the north, another in the south, another in the east, and another in the west, will be brought together again in the twinkling of an eye, and our spirits will take possession of them. We shall then be prepared to dwell with the Father and the Son, and we never can be prepared to dwell with them until then. Spirits, when they leave their bodies, do not dwell with the Father and the Son, but live in the Spirit world, where there are places prepared for them...This body must be changed, else it cannot be prepared to dwell in the glory of the Father. To me all these things are plain and easy [to understand]."[126]

Truly, choice doctrines were revealed by the Lord's chosen prophet. In another discourse, President Young revealed additional information.

ADDITIONAL TEACHINGS

On August 24, 1872, President Young delivered teachings to a congregation of members of the Church in Farmington, Utah. In one part of his discourse, he said: "It is twenty-eight years since Brother Joseph [Smith] was killed, and the work has gone forth steadily and rapidly, and through the providences of God we have apparently advanced faster since then...The work is still [moving] onward, and it is upward."

Later, he said: "Now a few words to the brethren and sisters upon the doctrine and ordinances of the house of God [the temple]. All who have lived on the earth according to the best light they had, and would have received the fullness of the Gospel had it been preached to them, are worthy of a glorious resurrection, and will attain to this by being administered for in the flesh by those who have the authority. All others will have a resurrection, and receive a glory, except those who have sinned against the Holy Ghost.

[Note these words:] "It is supposed by this people [members of the Church] that we have all the ordinances in our possession for life and salvation, and exaltation, and that we are administering in these ordinances. This is not the case. We are in possession of all the ordinances that can be administered in the flesh; but there are other ordinances and administrations that must be administered beyond this world. I know you would ask what they are. I will mention one. *We have not, neither can we receive here, the ordinance and the keys of the resurrection.* [Again, note these words:] They will be given to those who have passed off this stage of action and have received their bodies again [by the resurrection], as many have already done and many more will. *They will be ordained* [evidently by the laying on of hands upon their heads], *by those who hold the keys of the resurrection, to go forth and resurrect the Saints,* just as we receive the ordinance of baptism, then the keys of authority to baptize others for the remission of their sins. *This is one of the ordinances we cannot receive here* [on earth], *and there are many more."* [127]

Praise be given to God for allowing his chosen servant to share this insightful doctrine. This will truly be a choice event to experience and witness! More about this teaching will be given later.

ELDER WILFORD WOODRUFF

In one of his many journals, then Elder Wilford Woodruff, of the Quorum of the Twelve Apostles, who later was set apart as the fourth president of the Church, wrote the following: "Who will resurrect Joseph [Smith's] body?" Answering his own question, he wrote: "It will be [either] Peter, [or] James, [or] John, [or] Moroni, or someone who has or will *receive the keys of the resurrection.* It will probably be one of those who hold the keys of this dispensation and has delivered them to Joseph and you will see Jesus and he will eat peaches and apples with you. But the world will not see it or know of it for wickedness will increase. Joseph and Jesus will be there. They will walk and talk with them [individuals who will be given keys of the resurrection] at times and no man mistrusts who they are [because they will be honorable]. Joseph will lead the Armies of Israel whether he is seen or no, whether visible or invisible as seemeth him good.

[Note these words:] *"Joseph has got to receive the keys of the resurrection for you and I.* After he is resurrected he will go and resurrect Brother Brigham [Young], Brother Heber [C. Kimball, a counselor in the First Presidency to President Young], and Brother [Don] Carlos [who was the Prophet Joseph's Smith's righteous brother who died when he was age twenty-five], and when that is done then He will say, "now go [forth] Brother Brigham and resurrect your wives and children and gather them together. While this is done, the wicked will know nothing of it...This is the way the resurrection will be. All will not be raised at once but will continue in this way until all the righteous are resurrected.

"After Joseph Smith comes to us in his resurrected body, He will more fully instruct us concerning the baptism for the dead and the sealing ordinances. He will say, be baptized for this man and that man [mankind] and [for additional mankind] to be sealed [vicariously in a temple]...and connect the Priesthood together. I tell you there will not be much of this done until Joseph comes."
128

Thanks be given to Elder Wilford Woodruff for writing these fascinating doctrines! This truly will be a joyous day for those individuals who have spent considerable time in the spirit world anticipating having these required gospel ordinances performed.

Elder Boyd K. Packer, of the Quorum of the Twelve Apostles, wrote these praising words: "If I were to describe President Woodruff in one word that would best characterize him, I would choose the word *spirituality*. A man of deep spiritual attunement, from the days of his youth he had received and responded to spiritual guidance; and it was this trait, perhaps above any other, that qualified him for a call to be a member of the Quorum of the Twelve Apostles." [129]

PRESIDENT SPENCER W. KIMBALL

We now turn our attention to the year 1977. In the Priesthood Session of the April General Conference of The Church of Jesus Christ of Latter-day Saints, President Spencer W. Kimball, twelfth president of the Church began his discourse by quoting President Brigham Young, the second president of this dispensation: "'It is supposed by this people that we have all the ordinances in our possession for life and salvation, and exaltation, and that we are administering in those ordinances.

This is not the case. We are in possession of all the ordinances that can be administered in the flesh; but there are other ordinances and administrations that must be administered beyond this world. I know you would like to ask what they are. I will mention one. We have not, neither can we receive here, the ordinance and the keys of resurrection.' (*Journal of Discourses*, 15:137.)

This quotation testifies to this author that living prophets spend time studying the teachings of early apostles and prophets.

President Kimball then asked two questions: "*Do we have the keys of resurrection?* Could you return to the earth as ones who would never again die—your own parents, your grandparents, your ancestors?

"I buried my mother when I was eleven, my father when I was in my early twenties. I have missed my parents much. [Note these words:] *If I had the power of resurrection as did the Savior of the world, I would have been tempted to try to have kept them longer.*

"I have been called to speak in numerous funerals for people whom I have known, people whom I have loved, and people whom I have saved and held on to in a limited way. We do not know of anyone who can resurrect the dead as did Jesus the Christ when he came back to mortality...

He later reflects: "Perhaps there is something

else that we will learn as we perfect our bodies and our spirits in the times to come. You and I—what helpless creatures are we! Such limited power we have, and how little can we control the wind and the waves and the storms! We remember the numerous scriptures which, concentrated in a single line, were said by a former prophet, Lorenzo Snow: 'As man is, God once was; and as God is, man may become.' This is a power available to us as we reach perfection and receive the experience and power to create, to organize, to control native elements. How limited we are now! We have no power to force the grass to grow, the plants to emerge, the seeds to develop...

He again quotes: "'We have no such ordinance here,' said Brigham Young. 'We organize according to men in the flesh. By combining the elements and planting the seed, we cause vegetables, trees, grains, etc. to come forth.' But we do not give them life. 'We are organizing a kingdom here according to the pattern that the Lord has given for people in the flesh, but not for those who have received the resurrection, although it is a similitude.'" (*Journal of Discourses* 15:137.)

Near the end of his discourse, President Kimball stated: "We talk about the gospel in its fulness; yet we realize that a large part is still available to us as we prepare, as we perfect our lives, and as we become more like our God. Are we ready for it? In the Doctrine and Covenants we read of Abraham, who has already attained godhood. He has received many powers, undoubtedly, that we would like to have and will eventually get if we continue faithful and perfect our lives.

"My brethren, God bless you as we carry forward our lives toward perfection so that we may attain and receive the blessings that we are promised, that we may reach godhood eventually and have the blessings appertaining thereto." [130]

This author is so thankful for these choice teachings that were spoken by the Lord's chosen prophet at a General Conference of the Church.

ELDER BOYD K. PACKER

In one of his excellent writings, Elder Boyd K. Packer, of the Quorum of the Twelve Apostles, wrote this about President Kimball:

"I heard President Kimball say on one occasion, as other Presidents of the Church, that, while he holds all of the keys that are held upon the earth, there are keys that he does not hold. There are keys that have not been given to him as President of the Church, because they are reserved to higher power and authority. For instance, *he said that he does not hold the keys of the resurrection.* The Lord holds them, but He has not delegated them—neither anciently, nor to modern prophets...

Elder Packer then declares: "Nevertheless, in the Church we hold sufficient authority to perform all of the ordinances necessary to redeem and to exalt the whole human family. And, because we have keys to the sealing power, what we bind in proper order here will be bound in heaven. Those keys—the keys to seal and bind on earth, have it bound in heaven—represent the consummate gift from our God. With that authority we can baptize and bless, we can endow and seal, and the Lord will honor our commitments." [131]

These few words speak volumes of truth!

ELDER RUSSELL M. NELSON

We now turn to the April 1995 General Conference of The Church of Jesus Christ of Latter-day Saints. Then Elder Russell M. Nelson, of the Quorum of the Twelve Apostles, began his talk with these heart-felt words:

"The title of my message is the scriptural phrase 'children of the covenant.' In introducing this topic, I will reflect on recent events as a colleague of President Howard W. Hunter and as a father and upon earlier experiences as a doctor of medicine.

"These past weeks have been challenging for Sister Nelson and me. Not only have we bid farewell to our beloved President Hunter [fourteenth president of the Church], but thirty-three days earlier, we suffered the demise of our precious daughter Emily. A mother of five young children, Emily had just celebrated her thirty-seventh birthday when called to the other side.

"President Hunter influenced Emily's life in a real way. She welcomed his invitation for all adult members of the Church to hold a temple recommend. She and her husband, Bradley Wittwer, regarded their regular time in the temple as a sacred privilege. They viewed 'the temple of the Lord as the great symbol of their membership and the supernal setting for their most sacred covenants.' She strived to emulate the example of the Lord Jesus Christ. Even though illness brought intense suffering to President Hunter and Emily, an angry word never fell from their lips. Instead, they chose to endure with loving faith. When well-meaning friends and family expressed concern for Emily, she cheerfully replied, 'Don't worry, I'll be OK!' Even when she concluded a telephone call, she did not close with the customary 'good-bye.' She would say, 'I love you!'

"When President Boyd K. Packer and I last visited President Hunter, he beckoned for Sister Hunter, reached for her hand, and said with a smile, 'I feel better when you are near me.'

"*My tears of sorrow have flowed along with wishes that I could have done more for our daughter and for our*

President. If I had the power of resurrection, I would have been tempted to bring them back. Though one of the ordained Apostles, each of whom is entrusted with all the keys of the kingdom of God, I do not hold keys of the Resurrection. Jesus Christ holds those keys and will use them for Emily, for President Hunter, and for all people in the Lord's own time.

"Emily and President Hunter had no fear of death. They had made and honored sacred covenants with the Lord, and they knew that his covenants to them will be kept with equal fidelity. They lived nobly as 'children of the covenant'." [132]

It is worth emphasizing what Elder Nelson said, that *if he had the power of resurrection, he would have been tempted to bring back [to life] both President Hunter and his daughter, Emily.* With a sure testimony, he testified that *Jesus Christ holds those keys and will use them for Emily, for President Hunter, and for all people in the Lord's own time.*

As previously quoted, President Spencer W. Kimball, in 1977, spoke these words: "I buried my mother...[and] my father. I have missed my parents much. *If I had the power of resurrection... I would have been tempted to try to have kept them longer.*" [133]

Though eighteen years separated President Kimball's expressions from those of Elder Nelson's, it is this author's view that due to true love and loss, both servants of the Lord were inspired by the Holy Ghost to speak nearly identical wording.

CONCLUDING STATEMENTS

Summarizing what has been presented in this section on the keys of the resurrection, the following has been taught:

(1) In a patriarchal blessing, my son, Nathan, was told that Jesus Christ would bestow upon him *the keys of resurrection*, that he might bring his eternal helpmeet from the grave, based on his faithfulness.

(2) From two discourses given by President Brigham Young, he *first* taught that after the spirit leaves the body, it remains without a physical body in the spirit world until the Lord, by his law, brings to pass the resurrection of the dead. *When the angel who holds the keys of the resurrection shall sound his trumpet*, then the peculiar fundamental particles that organized our bodies here on earth will be brought together again in the twinkling of an eye, and our spirits will take possession of them.

Secondly, we are in possession of all the ordinances that can be administered in the flesh, but we have *not, neither can we receive here, the ordinance and the keys of the resurrection*. Later, they will be given to those who are resurrected, and *ordained to hold the keys of the resurrection,* to go forth and resurrect the Saints.

(3) In a journal entry by Elder Wilford Woodruff, he wrote that Joseph Smith would be resurrected and to *receive the keys of the resurrection for you and me,* then, to direct others to perform necessary gospel ordinances.

(4) In a General Conference, President Spencer W. Kimball said that he missed his parents, and if he had the power of resurrection, he would have been tempted to have kept them longer. He admonished the members of the Church to live worthy of receiving all the ordinances, which some will be given after mortal life.

(5) In a book written by Elder Boyd K. Packer, he wrote of President Kimball speaking as holding all the keys that are held on earth; however, there are other keys he did not hold, *one was the keys of resurrection.*

(6) In a General Conference, Elder Russell M. Nelson said that he was saddened by the passing of President Hunter and his daughter, Emily, and, if he had *the power of resurrection,* he would have been tempted to bring them back.

With these truths established, we now turn our attention to the glorious doctrine of resurrection.

First And Second Resurrection

WHILE IN MORTALITY, JESUS SPOKE THESE GREAT truths: "Marvel not at this: for the hour is coming, in the which all that are in the graves shall hear his voice, And shall come forth; they that have done good, unto the resurrection of life [meaning eternal life, exaltation]; and they that have done evil, unto the resurrection of damnation" [meaning that limits will be placed on their progression] (See John 5:28-29; See also Doctrine and Covenants 76:16-18).

Providing additional information, it is written in LDS beliefs: *"The first resurrection began when the risen Lord came forth from the tomb...*Among those who rose from the dead were Moses, Elijah,

Elias, John the Baptist, and the righteous Saints of Enoch's city of Zion (D&C 133:54-55). Later, Peter, James, the Book of Mormon prophet Moroni, and perhaps others were also resurrected.

"From the Doctrine and Covenants we learn that *at Christ's second coming, the first resurrection will resume* (D&C 29:11-13; 45:44-46; 88:95-98; 133:56). Latter-day Saints refer to this as the 'morning of the first resurrection'. . . . These are they who are resurrected and 'caught up to meet [the Savior] in the midst of the pillar of heaven' (D&C 88:97) and 'shall come forth and stand on the right hand of the Lamb, when he shall stand upon Mount Zion' (D&C 133:56). [Note these words:] The resurrection will continue throughout the Millennium as those who are mortal at Christ's coming and those who are born during the thousand years of peace and righteousness will live to 'the age of a tree' [which some surmise to be 100 years old] and then die and be resurrected in the 'twinkling of an eye' (D&C 101:30-32; see also Isaiah 65:17-20)." [134]

In another writing, the following was written by Gerald N. Lund, an emeritus General Authority:

"We also know from the scriptures that there will be a First and a Second resurrection…these two phrases describe an order in the Resurrection that is determined by our personal holiness and worthiness…Therefore, we know that the First Resurrection has two parts as far as timing goes. [Note these words:]

"For example, we know that *Joseph Smith and others of this dispensation are still in the spirit world teaching the gospel* (see D&C 138:53-54), which means that sometime after the resurrection of those who were resurrected with Christ, resurrection stopped for a time, and will not take place again until Christ comes.

[Again, note these words:] "How then do we explain the resurrection of the angel Moroni, who died about 400 years later? … [Answering] Joseph Fielding Smith reminds us of an important point: 'While the scriptures speak of the First Resurrection and the second… these expressions do not preclude the power and authority of our Lord to call forth from the dead any one whom he pleases without waiting for a general resurrection….' (Smith, *Answers to Gospel Questions*, 3:86)

"*The morning of the First Resurrection will resume just before Christ's coming…*

"The first to come forth from their graves will be those who have lived worthily enough to be exalted and go on to godhood, as described by the Lord: 'If ye receive me in the world, then shall ye know me, and shall receive your exaltation; that where I am ye shall be also. This is *eternal lives*.' (D&C 132:23-24). Eternal *lives*—plural—means that they will have the great privilege of creating spirit children just as our Heavenly Parents did.

"But we also know that there will be people who lived faithfully enough to allow them to go to the celestial kingdom even though they will not be gods but will be 'ministering servants' to those who are gods (see D&C 131:1-4; 132:16-17) …

"We should keep in mind here that 'morning' and 'afternoon' define an order of sequence of the Resurrection rather than a specific time…

"What we are told is that three groups will be resurrected immediately before or during the Millennium—those being exalted, those going to the celestial kingdom but not as exalted beings, and those going to the terrestrial kingdom. Beyond that we are not given more details…

"What follows in section 88 of the Doctrine and Covenants not only describes the First Resurrection but gives us more details on the Second—or last—Resurrection." [See verses 93-98; see also D&C 45]

THE SECOND RESURRECTION

In the Doctrine and Covenants, the following is written: "But, behold, verily I say unto you, before the earth shall pass away, *Michael [Adam], mine archangel shall sound his trump, and then shall*

all the dead awake, for their graves shall be opened, and they shall come forth [will be resurrected]—yea, even all" (88:26. Italics added). Thus, this is the final resurrection or defined as the Second Resurrection. And Adam will be a key figure commencing this event.

"The Second Resurrection will begin at the end of the Millennium and will be for those who are destined for telestial glory. They will have [had] to wait for another thousand years of earth time to come forth from their graves… Sons of perdition from this earth will also be resurrected, but only after all others have been (see D&C 76:37-39)…

"We shall close with President Joseph F. Smith's explanation: 'It is our duty to make ourselves acquainted with those laws, that we may know how to live in harmony with his will while we dwell in the flesh, that we may be entitled to come forth *in the morning of the First Resurrection, clothed with glory, immortality and eternal lives,* and be permitted to sit down at the right hand of God, in the kingdom of heaven. And except we become acquainted with those laws, and live in harmony with them, we need not to expect to enjoy these privileges (Joseph F. Smith, *Gospel Doctrine,* 435)." [135]

ADDITIONAL TEACHINGS

With the First and Second Resurrection completed, the effects of the fall of Adam and Eve are swallowed up in Jesus Christ. All are brought back into the presence of God to be judged according to their individual righteousness. It is written in the Book of Mormon that, by the power of God and by virtue of our Savior's infinite atonement, all mankind—both righteous and wicked—will be resurrected to immortality. Death will be forever destroyed (See 2 Nephi 9:10-13).

The Prophet Joseph Smith saw in vision the resurrection and testified of the greatness of this marvelous event:

"Would you think it strange if I relate what I have seen in vision in relation to this interesting theme [of resurrection]? Those who have died in Jesus Christ may expect to enter into all the fruition of joy when they come forth, which they possessed or anticipated here.

"So plain was the vision, that *I actually saw men [mankind] before they had ascended from the tomb, as they were getting up slowly. They took each other by the hand and said to each other, 'My father, my son, my mother, my daughter, my brother, my sister.'* And when the voice calls for the dead to arise, suppose I am laid by the side of my father, what would be the first joy of my heart? To meet my father, my mother, my brother, my sister; and when they are at my side, *I embrace them and they me...*

"All your losses will be made up to you in the resurrection, provided you continue faithful. *By the vision of the Almighty I have seen it.*

"...The expectations of seeing my friends in the morning of the resurrection cheers my soul and makes me bear up against the evils of life..." 136

ABILITIES OF RESURRECTED BEINGS

Elder Bruce R. McConkie penned this great insight as to various abilities of resurrected beings: "From this brief review [of ten appearances of the resurrected Jesus Christ which was presented earlier in this work] We learn several important things: we know that resurrected beings, containing their glory with themselves, can walk as mortals do on earth; that they can converse and reason and teach as they once did in mortality; that they can both withhold and manifest their true identities; that they can pass with corporeal bodies through solid walls; that they have bodies of flesh and bones which can be felt and handled; that if need be (and at special times) they can retain the scars and wounds of the flesh; that they can eat and digest food; that they can vanish from mortal eyes and transport themselves by means unknown to us." [137]

In complete harmony with these teachings, Elder James E. Talmage, of the Quorum of the Twelve Apostles, wrote the following: "A resurrected body, though of tangible substance, and possessing all the organs of a mortal tabernacle, is not bound to earth by gravitation, nor can it be hindered in its movements by material barriers... But that resurrected beings move in accordance with laws making such passage possible and to them natural, is evidenced not only by the instance of the risen Christ, but by the movements of other resurrected personages. Thus, in September,1823, Moroni, the Nephite prophet who had died about 400 A.D., appeared to Joseph Smith in his chamber [bedroom], three times during one night, coming and going without hindrance incident to walls or roof, (see P. of G. P., Joseph Smith 2:43)...So also resurrected beings possess the power of rendering themselves visible or invisible to the physical vision of mortals." [138]

From what has been written about the abilities of resurrected beings, "that they can pass with corporeal bodies through solid walls," we are assured that all will easily pass through a coffin, dirt, or whatever, and come up out of the ground to greet family members and friends.

A VALID QUESTION

It is proper to ask about individuals who were never buried in a grave. What of those who have been drowned at sea, missing in wars, perished in fires, or a variety of other deaths?

To help answer, we turn to one of the teachings of President Brigham Young: "We are here in circumstances to bury our dead according to the order of the Priesthood. But some of our brethren [and sisters] die upon the ocean; they cannot be buried in a burying ground, but they are sewed upon in canvas and cast into the sea, and perhaps two minutes after they are in the bowels of the shark, yet those persons will come forth in the resurrection, and receive all the glory of which they are worthy, and be clothed upon with all the beauty of resurrected Saints, as much so as if they had been laid away in a gold or silver coffin, and in a place expressly for burying the dead." [139]

In the Book of Mormon, Alma provides this great comfort: "The soul shall be restored to the body, and the body to the soul; yea, and every limb and joint shall be restored to its body; yea, *even a hair of the head shall not be lost*; but all things shall be restored to their proper and perfect frame" (Alma 40:23; see also 11:44. Italics added).

By spiritual laws not revealed, the body and the soul will be restored. Nothing is lost or misplaced by God the Father and His Son, Jesus Christ. As to individuals who are not buried in graves, it has not been revealed where they will be resurrected. The hope of this author is that they will be resurrected by friends or relatives so they can embrace one another, as was shown in vision to the Prophet Joseph Smith.

Alma, the Book of Mormon prophet, revealed enlightened details about life after physical death. He wrote these words: "Now, there is a death which is called a temporal death; and the death of Christ shall loose the bands of this temporal death, that all shall be raised from this temporal death. The spirit and body shall be reunited again in its perfect form; both limb and joint shall be restored to its proper frame, even as we now are at this time; and we shall be brought to stand before God, knowing even as we know now, and have a bright recollection of all our guilt.

[Note these words:] "Now, this restoration shall come to all, both old and young, both bond and free, both male and female, both the wicked and the righteous; and even there shall not so much as a hair of their heads be lost; but everything shall be restored to its perfect frame, as it is now, or in the body, and shall be brought and be arraigned before the bar of Christ the Son, and God the Father, and the Holy Spirit, which is one Eternal God [meaning a oneness of perfection], to be judged according to their works, whether they be good or whether they be evil.

"Now, behold, I have spoken unto you concerning the death of the mortal body, and also concerning the resurrection of the mortal body. I say unto you that this mortal body is raised to an immortal body, that is from death, even from the first death of life, that they can die no more; their spirits uniting with their bodies, never to be divided; thus the whole becoming spiritual and immortal, that they can no more see corruption." (Alma 11:42-45).

Elder Russell M. Nelson explained this well: "Knowledge of the resurrection of the dead presents to the informed mind enlightened concepts of hope, love, and joy. The appreciation of that glorious state almost defies description. John the Revelator wrote of his vision of the possibility of our eventual reunion with the Savior of the world: 'And God shall wipe away all tears from their eyes; and there shall be no more death, neither sorrow, nor crying, neither shall there be any more pain: for the former things are passed away'" (Revelation 21:4). [140]

JOYFUL REUNIONS

Regarding departed loved ones, this event can be compared to the anticipation of family members and friends anxiously awaiting the arrival of a newborn baby. Likewise, family and friends anxiously awaiting and embracing a released missionary who has been away for a year or two. In addition, going to a family reunion and seeing and conversing with loved ones that have not been seen for a considerable amount of time. There are a variety of anticipated events, but all result in a happy and joyous association.

Elder Nelson had well-written: "When those who weep for the loss of a loved one are fully able to comprehend these concepts, their tears of separation may literally be turned to tears of anticipation. Joyful reunions await those who prepare for them." [141]

Concluding this work, the author sincerely hopes the reader feels assured concerning the inevitable event called death and senses the peace of God, looking forward to a glorious resurrection, and a joyful reunion with loved ones—especially with our Heavenly Father and our Elder Brother, Jesus Christ.

<u>Endnotes</u>

1   Russell M. Nelson, *The Gateway We Call Death* (Salt Lake City: Deseret Book Co., 1995), 1-8.

2   Brigham Young, in *Journal of Discourses*, 26 vols. (London: Latter-day Saints' Book Depot, 1854-86), 8:28. Italics added. The word *scriptures* have been modernized.

3   Heber C. Kimball, in *Journal of Discourses*, 10:100. Italics added.

4   Wilford Woodruff, in *Journal of Discourses*, 22:348. Italics added.

5   Orson F. Whitney, in *Young Women's Journal*, (Salt Lake City, April 1928), 39:204. Italics added.

6   Joseph F. Smith, in *Juvenile Instructor*, June 1, 1905, 40:336. Italics added.

7   Franklin D. Richards, An Address, October 9, 1887, *Collected Discourses*, 84; Volume 1, 1886-1889. Italics added.

8   Paul H. Dunn and Richard M. Eyre, *The Birth We Call Death* (Salt Lake City: Aspen Books, 1999), pp. 5, 11, 26. "Originally published; *The Birth That We Call Death*, (Salt Lake City: Bookcraft, 1976)."

9   Ibid., 10-11.

10 Joseph Smith, *Teachings of the Prophet Joseph Smith*, sel. by Joseph Fielding Smith (Salt Lake City: Deseret Book Co., 1976), 310.

11 *LDS Beliefs, A Doctrinal Reference* (Salt Lake City: Deseret Book Co., 2011), 474. Italics added.

12 Bruce R. McConkie, *A New Witness for the Articles of Faith* (Salt Lake City: Deseret Book Co., 1985), 157-58. Italics

added.

13 Brigham Young, in *Journal of Discourses*, 3:372. Italics added.

14 Parley P. Pratt, *Key to the Science of Theology*, 3rd edition, (Salt Lake City: Deseret News, 1883), 129-130. Italics added.

15 Harold B. Lee, "Funeral Services for Mable Hale Forsey," October 24, 1960; typewritten copy, page 12. Italics added.

16 Alvin R. Dyer, *Who Am I?* (Salt Lake City: Deseret Book Co., 1963), 501-502. Italics added.

17 Russell M. Nelson, *The Gateway We Call Death*, (Salt Lake City: Deseret Book Co., 1995), 81. Italics added.

18 Brigham Young, in *Journal of Discourses*, 8:30. Italics added.

19 Ibid., 8:30. Italics added.

20 Orson Hyde, in *Journal of Discourses*, 8:25. Italics added.

21 Brigham Young, in *Journal of Discourses*, 8:30. Italics added.

22 *A Commentary On The Holy Bible* (commonly referred to as *The One-Volume Bible Commentary*), edited by The Reverend J.R. Dummelow; Copyright renewed 1936, (New York: The Macmillan Company, 1970), 400.

23 The Silver Cord And The Near-Death Experience, by Kevin Williams, September 22, 2019; See https://near-death.com.silver-cord/.

24 Orson Hyde, in *Journal of Discourses*, 8:26. Italics added.

25 Brigham Young, in *Journal of Discourses*, 26 vols. 8:30. Italics added.

26 Joseph Smith, *Teachings of the Prophet Joseph Smith*, 196-97.

27 Russell M. Nelson, *The Gateway We Call Death*, 40-41.

28 Joseph F. Smith, *Gospel Doctrine: Selections from the Sermons and Writings of Joseph F. Smith* (Salt Lake City: Deseret Book, 1973), 452-54.

29 Joseph Smith, *Teachings of the Prophet Joseph Smith*, 107.

30 Joseph Fielding Smith, *Doctrines of Salvation*, comp. Bruce R. McConkie, 3 vols. (Salt Lake City: Bookcraft, 1954-56), 2:53.

31 Joseph F. Smith, *Gospel Doctrine*, 452.

32 Orson Pratt, *The Seer*, Washington, DC edition, (March 1853) 1, [No.3], 36.

33 Heber C. Kimball, in *Journal of Discourses*, 4:135-136.

34 Joseph F. Smith, *Gospel Doctrine*, 455.

35 Ibid., 455.

36 Bryant S. Hinckley, *Sermons and Missionary Services of Melvin J. Ballard*, 18th ed. (Salt Lake City: Deseret Book, 1973), 260.

37 Joseph F. Smith, *Gospel Doctrine*, 455-56.

38 Ibid., 456-457.

39 Joseph Fielding Smith, *Doctrines of Salvation*, 2:56. Italics added.

40 Ibid., 2:293. Italics added.

41 Ibid., 2:292.

42 Joseph Fielding Smith, *Doctrines of Salvation*, 3:65.

43 David J. Ridges, *The Gospel Study Series, Your Study of The Book of Mormon Made Easier, Part 3*: Helaman through Moroni (Springville, UT: Cedar Fort, 2007), 348.

44 Russell M. Nelson, *The Gateway We Call Death*, 46-47.

45 Brigham Young, in *Journal of Discourses*, 17:143.

46 Ibid., 17:143.

47 Joseph Fielding Smith, *Doctrines of Salvation*, 2:280.

48 Ibid., 2:281.

49 Joseph Smith, *Teachings of the Prophet Joseph Smith*, 296.

50 Ibid., pp. 215-16).

51 Russell M. Nelson, *The Gateway We Call Death*, 50-51.

52 Ibid., 52-53.

53 Orson F. Witney, In Conference Reports of The Church of Jesus Christ of Latter-day Saints (Salt Lake City: The Church of Jesus Christ of Latter-day Saints, 1898 to present), April 1929, 110-11.

54 Russell M. Nelson, *The Gateway We Call Death*, 54.

55 Ibid., 55.

56 In possession of the author.

57 Russell M. Nelson, *The Gateway We Call Death*, 59-63.

58 Ibid., 63.

59 Ezra Taft Benson, First Presidency's Christmas Devotional, December 7, 1986.

60 Joseph Smith, *Teachings of the Prophet Joseph Smith*, 106-107. (See also *History of the Church* 2:380-381).

61 Heber C. Kimball, in *Journal of Discourses*, 4:135-136.

62 Francis M. Gibbons, *Dynamic Disciples, Prophets of God: Life Stories of the Presidents of The Church of Jesus Christ of Latter-day Saints,* (Salt Lake City: Deseret Book Co., 1996), 127. From "Talking Scripture." Copy in author's possession. He has taken sections from LeRoi C. Snow, "Raised from the Dead," *Improvement Era*, Vol. 32, No. 11, September 1929.

63 LeRoi C. Snow, "Raised from the Dead," *Improvement Era*, Vol. 32, No. 11, September 1929, 883.

64 Joseph F. Smith, *Gospel Doctrine*, 455.

65 Francis M. Gibbons, *Dynamic Disciples, Prophets of God: Life Stories of the Presidents of The Church of Jesus Christ of Latter-day Saints,* 127.

66 James E. Faust, An Address, October 5, 1972, at a Regional Representatives Seminar, 1.

67 Russell M. Nelson, *The Gateway We Call Death*, 102.

68 Ibid., 66.

69 Spencer W. Kimball, "Tragedy or Destiny," *Improvement Era*, March 1966, 178.

70 Russell M. Nelson, *The Gateway We Call Death*, 68.

71 Ibid., 69.

72 Bruce R. McConkie, *Mormon Doctrine*, 2nd ed. (Salt Lake City: Bookcraft, 1966), 771.

73 Bruce R. McConkie, *Doctrinal New Testament Commentary,* 3 vols. (Salt Lake City: Bookcraft, 1965-73) 2:440-441.

74 Bruce R. McConkie, *Mormon Doctrine*, 2nd ed. (Salt Lake City: Bookcraft, 1966), 828.

75 George Q. Cannon, of the First Presidency; An Address,

October 4, 1892, and written in *The Millennial Star* 55:61, January 23. 1893.

76 M. Russell Ballard, "Suicide: Some Things We Know, and Some We Do Not," *Ensign*, October 1987. (Read the entire article).

77 Russell M. Nelson, *The Gateway We Call Death*, 72-73.

78 Ibid., 73-74.

79 Ibid.,73-77.

80 Bruce R. McConkie, *Mormon Doctrine*, 2nd ed. (Salt Lake City: Bookcraft, 1966), 594. Italics added.

81 Ibid., 594-595. Italics added.

82 *LDS Beliefs: A Doctrinal Reference*, (Salt Lake City: Deseret Book Co., 2011), 632.

83 Ibid., 632.

84 Ibid., 3:67, Notes 1.

85 Bruce R. McConkie, *Doctrinal New Testament Commentary*, 3 vols., (Salt Lake City: Bookcraft, Inc., 1972), 1:402.

86 Bruce R. McConkie, *The Mortal Messiah: From Bethlehem to Calvary*, 4 vols. (Salt Lake City: Deseret Book Co., 1980), 3:55.

87 Ibid., 3:56.

88 Bruce R. McConkie, *Mormon Doctrine*, 2nd ed. (Salt Lake City: Bookcraft, 1966), 803.

89 Bruce R. McConkie, *Doctrinal New Testament Commentary*, 3 vols., (Salt Lake City: Bookcraft, Inc., 1972), 1:400.

90 Bruce R. McConkie, *The Mortal Messiah: From Bethlehem to Calvary*, 4 vols. (Salt Lake City: Deseret Book Co., 1980), 3:57.

91 Joseph Fielding Smith, *Doctrines of Salvation*, comp. Bruce R. McConkie, 3 vols. (Salt Lake City: Bookcraft, 1954-56), 2:111.

92 Bruce R. McConkie, *Doctrinal New Testament Commentary*, 3 vols., (Salt Lake City: Bookcraft, Inc., 1972), 1:400.

93 Ibid., 1:400.

94 Ibid. 1:400. Italics added.

95 Ibid., 1:401. Wording and Italics added.

96 Bruce R. McConkie, *The Mortal Messiah: From Bethlehem to Calvary*, 4 vols. (Salt Lake City: Deseret Book Co., 1980), 3:59.

97 https://www.thefreedictionary.com/wattle

98 Bruce R. McConkie, *The Mortal Messiah: From Bethlehem to Calvary*, 4 vols. (Salt Lake City: Deseret Book Co., 1980), 3:61-62. Italics added by this author.

99 Bruce R. McConkie, *A New Witness for the Articles of Faith*, (Salt Lake City: Deseret Book Co., 1985), 321.

100 Ibid., 321-322.

101 James E. Talmage, *Jesus the Christ* (Salt Lake City: Deseret Book Co.,1962), 660. In the public domain.

102 Frederic W. Farrar, *The Life of Christ*, (Portland, Oregon: Fountain Publications, 1980), 672. In the public domain.

103 James E. Talmage, *Jesus the Christ* (Salt Lake City: Deseret Book Co.,1962), 662. In the public domain.

104 Frederic W. Farrar, *The Life of Christ*, (Portland, Oregon: Fountain Publications, 1980), 657-658. In the public domain.

105   Alfred Edersheim, *The Life and Times of Jesus the Messiah*, (New York, also London and Bombay: Longman's, Green, and Co. 1896), 2:617-618. In the public domain.

106   James E. Talmage, *Jesus the Christ,* (Salt Lake City: Deseret Book Co.,1962), 664-665. In the public domain.

107   Bruce R. McConkie, *The Mortal Messiah,* (Salt Lake City: Deseret Book Co., 1981), 4:261-262.

108   James E. Talmage, *Jesus the Christ* (Salt Lake City: Deseret Book Co.,1962), 680-681. In the public domain.

109   Bruce R. McConkie, *The Mortal Messiah* (Salt Lake City: Deseret Book Co., 1981), 4:264-265.

110   *LDS Beliefs, A Doctrinal Reference*, (Salt Lake City: Deseret Book Co., 2011), 532.

111   Bruce R. McConkie, "Gaining a Testimony of Jesus Christ," *Liahona*, July 1981.

112   Ibid. Italics and bold lettering added by this author.

113   *Wilford Woodruff, History of His Life and Labors*, as recorded in his daily journals. Prepared for publication by Matthias F. Cowley, September, 1909. Reprinted by (Salt Lake City: Bookcraft, 7th Printing, 1978), 541. Italics added. In the public domain.

114   *Wilford Woodruff, History of His Life and Labors*, as recorded in his daily journals. Prepared for publication by Matthias F. Cowley, September, 1909. Reprinted by (Salt Lake City: Bookcraft, 7th Printing, 1978), 328. Italics added. In the public domain.

115   Mark A. Mathews, "Priesthood keys: What are

they and why do they matter?" *Meridian Magazine*, September 9, 2018. Used by permission; obtained on November 5, 2025 by an email.

116   *LDS Beliefs, A Doctrinal Reference*, (Salt Lake City: Deseret Book Co., 2011), 532.

117   Russell M. Nelson, *Heart of the Matter: What 100 years of living have taught me*, (Salt Lake City: Deseret Book Co., 2023), 193-194. Italics added by President Nelson.

118   https://www.churchofjesuschrist.org/study/scriptures/bd

119   https://www.churchofjesuschrist.org/study/scriptures/gs

120   David J. Ridges, *Your Study of The Doctrine and Covenants Made Easier, Part 3*, (Springville, UT, Cedar Fort, 2005), Section 110:12, page 149.

121   *LDS Beliefs, A Doctrinal Reference*, (Salt Lake City: Deseret Book Co., 2011), 18.

122   Joseph Smith, *History of The Church of Jesus Christ of Latter-day Saints*. Edited by B.H. Roberts. 7 vols. 2d ed. rev. Salt Lake City: The Church of Jesus Christ of Latter-day Saints, 1932-1951, (See 6:251-253).

123   Bruce R. McConkie, *A New Witness for the Articles of Faith*, (Salt Lake City: Deseret Book, 1985), 322. Italics added.

124   Bruce R. McConkie, Council of the Twelve, An Address, July 19, 1981, Provo Temple Workers Meeting, p. 24. Italics and underline added by this author.

125   Bruce R. McConkie, *The Mortal Messiah: From*

Bethlehem to Calvary, 4 vols. (Salt Lake City: Deseret Book Co., 1979, 1:32, Notes 7. Italics added.

126   Brigham Young, in *Journal of Discourses*, 8:27-28. Italics added.

127   Ibid., 15:136-137. Italics added.

128   Susan Staker, ed., *Waiting for the World's End: The Diaries of Wilford Woodruff*, pp. 168-169. See also Robert J. Matthew's, Selected Writings of Robert J. Matthews, chapter 44, "The Doctrine of Resurrection," pp. 505-525. As found on the Internet.

129   Boyd K. Packer, *The Holy Temple*, (Salt Lake City: Bookcraft., 1980), 189. Italics in quotation.

130   Spencer W. Kimball, "Our Great Potential," May 1977 *Ensign*, 49-51.

131   Boyd K. Packer, *The Holy Temple*, (Salt Lake City: Bookcraft., 1980), 151. Italics in quotation.

132   Russell M. Nelson, "Children of the Covenant," April 1995 General Conference of The Church of Jesus Christ of Latter-day Saints.

133   Spencer W. Kimball, "Our Great Potential," May 1977 *Ensign*, 49-51.

134   Ibid., 534-535. Italics added.

135   Gerald N. Lund, *The Second Coming of the Lord*, (Salt Lake City: Deseret Book Co., 2020), 362-370. Italics added by Gerald Lund.

136   Joseph Smith, *History of The Church of Jesus Christ of Latter-day Saints*, ed. B.H. Roberts, 2d ed. rev. 7 vols. (Salt Lake City: The Church of Jesus Christ of Latter-day Saints,

1932-51), 5:361-362. Italics added. In the public domain.

137   Bruce R. McConkie, "Gaining a Testimony of Jesus Christ," *Liahona*, July 1981.

138   James E. Talmage, *Jesus the Christ* (Salt Lake City: Deseret Book Co.,1962), 698, Notes 1. In the public domain.

139   Brigham Young, in *Journal of Discourses*, 26 vols. (London: Latter-day Saints' Book Depot), (1854-86), 9:193. Italics added. In the public domain.

140   Russell M. Nelson, *The Gateway We Call Death*, 87.

141   Ibid. 88.